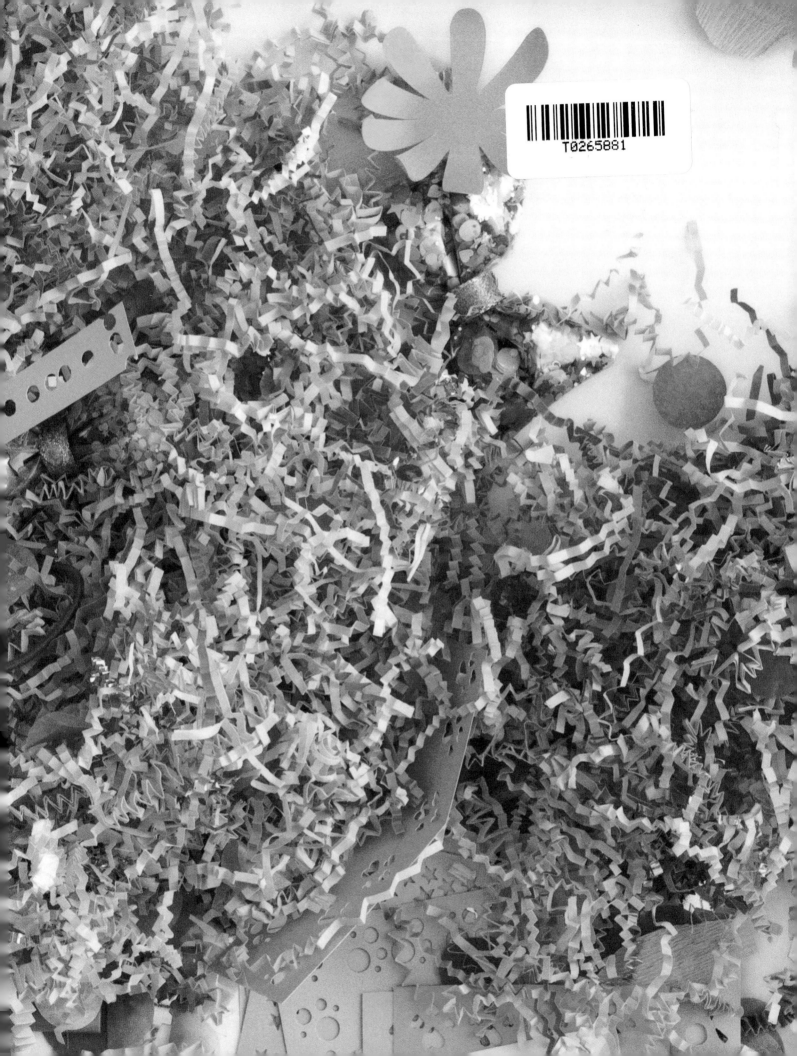

THE BIG BOOK OF
happy crafts

THE BIG BOOK OF
happy crafts

24 Creative Projects to Infuse Your World with Style, Personality & Fun

LUCIA MALLEA

BETTER DAY BOOKS®

HAPPY · CREATIVE · CURATED

Easy Templates Download!

Download all the ready-to-use templates for the projects in this book at the following link. All these templates are already included in the book, but if you need extras or simply don't want to remove pages, you can print the templates at home!

www.betterdaybooks.com/big-book-of-happy-crafts-templates-download

The Big Book of Happy Crafts © 2023
by Lucia Mallea and Better Day Books, Inc.

Publisher: Peg Couch
Book Designers: Lori Malkin Ehrlich and Llara Pazdan
Cover Designer: Ashlee Wadeson
Editor: Colleen Dorsey
Photographer: Gaby Di Pietro
Art Stylist: Pato Katz

Library of Congress Control Number: 2023932644

ISBN: 978-0-7643-6711-3
Printed in China
10 9 8 7 6 5 4 3 2 1

Copublished by Better Day Books, Inc., and Schiffer Publishing, Ltd.

Better Day Books

Better Day Books
P.O. Box 21462
York, PA 17402
Phone: 717-487-5523
Email: hello@betterdaybooks.com
www.betterdaybooks.com
@better_day_books

Schiffer Publishing
4880 Lower Valley Road
Atglen, PA 19310
Phone: 610-593-1777
Fax: 610-593-2002
Email: info@schifferbooks.com
www.schifferbooks.com

This title is available for promotional or commercial use, including special editions. Contact info@schifferbooks.com for more information.

To my dearest mom, who has been my source of inspiration. Your gentle guidance and support made all the difference in my life. Siempre en mi corazón.

To my husband, George, your encouragement has given me the courage to pursue my passion.

And to my kids, Benjamin, Isabel, and Julia, may you craft a beautiful life with love, purpose, and joy.

contents

Welcome! 8
Meet the Author 10
Studio Tour 12
Getting Started 14

projects

décor 24
Toucan Carioca 26
Leaf Wreath 32
Palm Leaves 38
Tropical Chandelier 44
Statement Stars 50
Paper Chandelier 54
Flower Curtain 60

party 64
Cake Stand 66
Confetti Candles 72
Party Crown 76
Party Poppers 82
Butterfly Crown 88

flowers 92
Cherry Blossoms 94
Giant Flower 100
Forever Plant 106
Poppies 112
Sunflowers 118

style 124
Confetti Purse 126
Flower Shoes 132
Parrot Earrings 138
Banana Fan 144
Confetti Shoe Bows 150
Upcycled Wallet 156
Heart Scrunchies 162

fun stuff

Templates 168
Index 183
Pullout Goodies 184

112

144

76

26

118

106

138

welcome!

I wrote a book! Or should I say, I crafted a book?

This experience has been amazing, to say the least. It all started with the news of our third baby coming. (Wow—I got to "bake" a book and a baby at the same time!) Choosing which projects to share with you was one of the hardest parts of making this book, because I love creating and experimenting with a little bit of everything—from paint to clay to yarn to paper crafts, you name it, I'll explore it. I focused on crafts with paper elements in this book because paper is a great and easy place to start! But I also brought in lots of fun additional materials to really engage your creativity. The projects are super varied in terms of their function—it's not all just decoration!—and time commitment—some projects will whip up in an hour and others will require a few hours of tracing and cutting. But all the projects are full of fun and color and—I hope—will bring you joy!

It was a bit of a challenge for this proCRAFTinator to make this book happen, but hey—we did it! And I say "we" because it took an army of friends, family, crafters, photographers, stylists, and supporters like you, the reader, to make it happen. It took longer to get this book into your hands than it did to get my new daughter into the world (hello, Julia!), but it was so worth it.

Join me on this journey of happy crafting!

meet the author

Where are you from, and where do you call home?

I was born in Argentina, have been moving around since I was five, and currently live in Miami, Florida. Being the daughter of a diplomat, I've been lucky enough to experience the amazing adventure that it is to live overseas. From Spain to Uruguay to the US to Brazil, it has been incredible experiences all around. My heart, however, has always been back in Argentina, where my extended family and friends are, and I still consider it home.

After many years moving around, I decided that after college I wanted to stay put in Argentina and have my forever life there. But, as you probably know, life can have a great sense of humor, because only a couple of years after activating my life master plan, I met an American named George, who would later become my husband, at a hostel in Mexico City. So, yeah . . . so much for that!

Since we've been together, we've lived all around and made beautiful memories and friendships with people from all over the world. I still call Argentina my home, but I would say I can make a happy life wherever we are, as long as we're together! (Bonus points if "wherever" includes *alfajores* and direct flights to Buenos Aires.)

How did you first get into crafting?

My mom was an amazing artist. She had this incredible sensitivity to art that I just loved to admire from a young age. She was a free spirit, and she always encouraged me to connect with what made me happy.

I remember the first project we did together. I had to show the pollination process for a school project in fourth grade. We created a giant paper flower and made paper bees around it. I remember how much joy it brought me not only to create something with my hands, but also to share it with someone I loved.

Crafting was basically my thing after that. Every birthday, when my friends were asking for Barbies, I was asking for blow markers or glow-in-the-dark paint. When everyone else was outside playing, my cousins and I were making handmade bracelets for our house-front store.

How does your Argentinian background affect your art style?

When I was little, you could find pretty much anything crafty in Argentina. Gold glitter paper with hot pink specks? Got it. Neon blue elastic bands with yellow polka dots? Got that too. At some point, though, things changed, and very specific items got replaced by very boring, generic ones.

Craft-wise, that's when things got interesting for me: if I wanted that gold glitter paper with hot pink specks, well, I had to make it myself. And I actually enjoyed the challenge. Rather than being frustrated, I was fired up and inspired to give my imagination and creativity free rein.

When you find yourself in this wonderful situation, you learn to look at things with fresh eyes. Everything has the possibility to become something else. Everything can be transformed. And I always thought that was magical.

What advice can you give readers who want to spend more time in the craft room?

Find something you are excited about, and you'll find yourself wanting to make it! It sounds pretty obvious, but I think that's exactly how it works.

How do you make a living from your art?

I create content for numerous brands that I love. I focus on producing super-easy tutorials, because I believe crafting should be fun, enjoyable, and as frustration-free as possible. I love my work because I'm always doing

it's me! hola :)

something different. I get to use different media and tools—from clay to special scissors and more—and it's the perfect job for someone who seeks out a new adventure every day!

Your work exudes such joy. What do you love most about crafting?

Being able to create with my hands. Transforming nothing into something. Making a unique object that says something about me—who I am, what I like, how I vibe, etc. I also love how there's no right or wrong with crafting. It's all about expressing yourself and having fun.

What are your favorite things to craft?

I love to craft a little bit of everything, but if I had to choose, I would say paper crafting is my favorite. Paper is so wonderful to work with and so versatile. It still blows me away how something so flat and lifeless can be turned into something so full of energy and life.

Besides crafting, what are your passions?

Learning new things—from a new technique to a new language, I love to be in constant movement and learning and exploring all the time. I don't feel like I have to be an expert on anything, but I do love to get a little glimpse of everything I can. I just wish I could clone myself so that I could get through that (neverending, really) to-do list!

How can we learn more about you?

I'm very active on Instagram (@luciamallea), which is where you can find most of my work. I'm also on TikTok (@soylumallea) and Pinterest (@lumallea). Hopefully, this will be the year when you can find me on YouTube too!

What do you hope readers get from this book?

Joy, joy, joy. I want you to have fun and connect with your creativity freely! I want you to let go of "should be"s and allow yourself to be amazed by what you can do.

Lucia Mallea is a dynamic bilingual content creator who has captured the hearts of over 300,000 followers worldwide with her vibrant art projects and accessible craft tutorials. She has collaborated with some of the world's most recognized brands, including Disney, Starbucks, Sharpie, and Dove. Originally from Argentina, Lucia now lives in Miami, Florida, where she continues to inspire crafters with her playful designs, creative use of color, and a healthy dose of glitter! To learn more, visit **www.luciamallea.com** and **@luciamallea** on Instagram.

¡VAMOS A CRAFTEARLA!

welcome to my studio!

I like my workspace to be inviting, bright, fun, and—you guessed it—colorful! But it also must make sense and be organized. I really dislike wasting time. Looking for my blue tape for 20 minutes will take me straight out of my happy place. Over the years, I've learned that having (and keeping!) my studio organized goes a long way. I give myself time to put things back after each project, but I know that the sooner I do it, the easier it will be for me to tackle the next project.

Natural light is another super-mega plus for me. I love working in it and filming in it, which, sometimes, I admit, can give me a headache, especially with these crazy Miami skies! But nothing beats it—having a bright space with plenty of windows and natural light is just magical.

getting started

In this section, I share tips for fun and frustration-free crafting as well as my recommendations for how to bring your own creativity and self-expression to the forefront in your work. After all, this book is not just a craft book—it's a book about happy crafts! May the projects and the process bring you tons of joy.

crafty tools and materials

Scissors

If I had to pick only three things to bring with me to a desert island, scissors would be one of them for sure (along with Diet Coke and Nerds, of course). A good pair of scissors can make all the difference in your final product, and, more importantly, in your crafting process.

We craft for joy, to have that magical moment of creativity spark into full power. Even though there are always panic moments when crafting, in general, crafting is supposed to be enjoyable and fun. And the wrong choice of craft materials or tools can make things a little cray cray.

Scissors come in all shapes, blades, and sizes. Just like you wouldn't paint with confetti or erase with a banana, there are specific scissors for specific materials. Some are pretty, some are utilitarian, and it's up to you to discover which works best with each material. The product packaging will usually give you a solid summary, but don't forget to experiment and figure them out for yourself. Take care of your scissors and try to keep them as faithful to their lovers as you can—reserve your paper scissors for paper, your cardboard scissors for cardboard, and so on.

Glue

Another thing I could not live without as a crafter is glue. Over the years I've become a big lover of hot glue guns. They might burn your fingers if you're not careful, but they will get everything done so much faster! I'm not a big fan of waiting forever for my glue to dry, so even though many of the projects in this book include the use of regular glue, you can often swap it out for hot glue if you'd prefer. I

recommend purchasing a small high-low-temperature glue gun. I can almost promise she'll be your new best friend! I even carry one in my purse—no joke.

Paper

The papers you use in your projects will make all the difference in how your final craft comes out. Yes, that's how much power they have! They can turn something eh into something WOW.

There are dozens of different types of papers; cardstock is my favorite, and it's a primary feature of many of the crafts in this book. Luckily, it's easy to find in any craft store. To start your collection, I recommend you get your hands on paper in a variety of colors and weights. There's nothing like a pretty rainbow of papers, so if you can create your own colorful collection, you'll never lack for inspiration.

Size-wise, standard 8½" x 11" (22 x 28 cm or A4) letter paper is sufficient for most projects. Sometimes you will need something a bit bigger and can grab 12" x 12" (31 x 31 cm) paper, or even 18" x 24" (46 x 61 cm) art papers.

Weight-wise, I prefer to use 65 lb/175 gram paper for most of my projects. It has a good firmness for substantial finished projects but is manageable in terms of flexibility and manipulation—you can get it to do what you want it to! For some specific projects, though, thinner paper is the name of the game—around 24 lbs/89 grams, which is similar to printer paper. Thinner paper can be a good choice when there is a lot of folding to do. Thicker paper tends to "break" when you fold it too many times.

Other Items

Scissors, glue, and paper: these are the three magic ingredients to most of my craft projects. But here are some other tools that I love and recommend that you get for your crafty journey:

- **Hole punch:** Find one that has multiple hole sizes and depth options.
- **Paper trimmer:** I can never cut straight!
- **Acrylic paint:** A basic set of vibrant colors will let you mix custom shades.
- **Glitter:** There is always room for this.
- **Ribbon and twine:** I like a nice gold and white baker's twine—it goes with everything!
- **Double-sided tape:** This is a must for quick and easy sticking!
- **Painter's tape or masking tape:** This is even great for crafting!

crazy about color

More is more and "less is a bore," to quote architect Robert Venturi, and I couldn't agree more! I like things to be big, bold, colorful, and over the top. Give me saturated rainbow colors, vibrant hues, glitter, sparkles, metallic fringe—you name it, I'll take it all!

Color simply makes me feel happy. Like a warm hug from a friend, a kitten cuddling on your lap, or an icy soda on a hot day, it gives an overall good feeling that makes me want to be around it—and I know I'm not alone in this sentiment. I love color in my projects, in my house, in my food, and in my clothes (which you'll see in the photos in this book!). I look for it all the time; consciously or unconsciously, I'm always choosing it.

Vibrant colors are my thing. You may have another palette that makes you feel all these things, and that is perfectly okay!

After all, we do need some balance in this world. Could you imagine how crazy it would be if everyone was obsessed with rainbow palettes like I am? We need those earth-tone lovers out there too to balance things out!

One fun thing I like to do to play with color is make color compositions using Pantone color cards, which are similar to paint sample cards. Each of the hundreds of possible colors is made up of a unique combination of hue, saturation, lightness, etc. I like to try to find trinkets around my house that match the card color and that are small enough to fit on the card.

I did a whole series of these that I'd love for you to check out. You can see them all on my website (*www.luciamallea.com/pantone*), and I also included some here as a teaser.

PANTONE® 18-2326
Cactus Flower

PANTONE® 17-1456
Tigerlily

PANTONE® 14-0852
Freesia

PANTONE® 18-4330
Swedish Blue

PANTONE
214

PANTONE
493

PANTONE 14-1911
Candy Pink

PANTONE
691

PANTONE
152

PANTONE 16-1255
Russet Orange

PANTONE 13-0850
Aspen Gold

PANTONE
142

PANTONE
605

PANTONE 13-0645
Limeade

PANTONE
7737

PANTONE
3278

PANTONE 18-4530
Celestial

PANTONE 18-4___
Caribbean Sea

PANTONE
291

PANTONE
9044

creativity and self-expression

The Maker's Mantra

In a world where more and more things are already manufactured, ready to use, or prepared for you, it's easy to feel discouraged about crafting. Why should I make something if it's already there to buy—and for just $1.99?

Yes, it happens—sometimes you'll end up buying what you want, and there's nothing wrong with that. But there's something magical about creating an item with your own hands—nothing compares to the joy you'll get out of crafting it yourself. Even if you spend five times the purchase cost in materials and dozens of hours and it doesn't come out as polished as the one you saw on the shelf, I promise there is still a reward to be gained from making it yourself.

Fueling Creativity

Creating can be so much fun! But creating *creatively* can be a little intimidating. That said, I believe everyone can be creative—the power is in you. Maybe you find your creativity in the kitchen, while whipping up delicious recipes, or in your personal approach to closet organization (Marie Kondo, is that you?), or somewhere else—I'm sure you can think of a way you are already creative. Still, how can you fuel that creativity and funnel it toward your crafting? Here are some ideas.

I love giving myself **fun challenges**. Sometimes I'll go into the supermarket for my regular grocery shopping and I'll say, okay, I need to choose three items and make a craft project with them. Give me that cereal box, a sponge, and . . . hmm . . . some salt. What can come out of that? No idea. But it's up to me to activate my creativity and just give it a try! There's no right or wrong here—it's a judgment-free zone—so just have fun and challenge yourself. Even if the outcome is a total bust, it'll still be a win because you activated your creativity and exercised that muscle.

you are creative
you are crafty
you are magical
and you hold the
power to make your
ideas come to life!

Another idea is to try to **look at things through different eyes**. Leave your expectations and assumptions behind you. Anything can become anything else. Your creativity has the power to transform a toilet brush into a beautiful miniature bottle-brush Christmas tree! Why not? The more you play around, the more ideas you'll get. In time, your brain just won't stop generating things to try!

Customize It!

This book is, of course, filled with ready-to-go projects, but the projects are also meant to give you ideas for how to create your own projects or personalize the ones here. Change the scale, have fun with color, or play with the paper: spray-paint it, dye it, stamp it, add texture by crunching it, add glitter to it, spray perfume on it to make it smell wonderful . . . Oh, the possibilities! Make it a whole experience, and you'll see how much fun you'll have.

Reusing and Upcycling

If you look around, you'll probably find a lot of gems you can craft with just lying around your house. I love upcycling things—I'm already thinking of what that laundry bottle can become before it's even halfway empty! I believe in recycling, reusing, reducing, and taking care of the materials I do buy. For example, no piece of pretty paper will end up in the trash after just a couple of cuts. I have a whole folder of scraps, organized by rainbow colors (of course), that I always go to before breaking out a fresh and whole piece of paper. And when a piece of paper finally becomes too cut-up or damaged? Well, then it becomes confetti!

Not only do I always look to reuse scraps, but a lot of my projects start from something that was formerly something else. For example, a Lucky Charms box went from holding delicious cereal to becoming a wallet that will hold millions of dollar bills. Don't they say there's a pot of gold at the end of those rainbows?

tips for fun and frustration-free crafting

Tidy Tools

Something that helps me craft a little more happily is when all my tools are ready to go. There's nothing that drives me crazier than sticky scissors or dirty markers. You know, like that time you were feeling Van Gogh–ish and painted yellow stars over blue skies with your markers, and now instead of having a yellow marker that colors yellow you have a yellow marker that colors green? Yeah . . .

So, as much as I dislike cleaning up after crafting, at some point, I learned that it'll only make me happier in future craft sessions—and I highly recommend it.

Getting Ready

Another thing I like to do before I craft is to reflect on the project I'm about to create. What color palette am I going to use? How will it make me feel to craft it? Is this a speedy project I'll get done in 30 minutes, or is this something I'm going to dedicate a bunch of mornings to? Is this a technique I am comfortable with? Am I feeling up for the challenge today, or should I shift to something more within my comfort zone? Will this be a gift for someone special, or is it something for myself? Where is it going to go once it's finished?

Of course, you don't have to ask yourself all these questions every time. Consider them food for thought. And, honestly, sometimes I just craft, zero questions asked.

Trusty Recommendations

- Make sure your scissors are clean and sharpened. Sticky and dull scissors can really gunk up a project.

- Keep yourself stocked up on the materials you use regularly. There's nothing more frustrating than being in the zone, only to realize you've run out of glue mid-stick.

- Invest in quality tools and materials: a good pair of scissors, a good hot glue gun, a good hole punch, nice paper, etc. This will be the only time you'll ever hear me tell you that less is more. Low-quality tools and materials will only bring you frustration.

- It can be very tempting to always buy the newest craft tool on the shelf. Try to remember that you don't need a million of them—again, prioritize quality over quantity.

Using the Templates

The templates are here to help you craft your projects in an easy way! For every project that has a template or templates, the templates are meant to be traced. I recommend that you trace each template shape on a piece of paper, cut them out, and then trace the shape onto something thicker, like a thin piece of cardboard (such as a cereal box). A thicker template will be easier to use, especially for complicated shapes or ones that you have to copy many times.

Sometimes I just ⚡✂️ CRAFT ! zero questions asked.

The template pages are perforated to make it easier to remove them. You can pull out an entire page and then photocopy or scan the templates from the book as a starting point. Remember, since the template pages are printed on both sides, don't cut out the template directly from the book page, or you'll ruin whatever template is on the other side of the page.

You can also download all the templates at the following link: *www.betterdaybooks.com/big-book-of-happy-crafts-templates-download*

Whatever option you choose, make sure to keep all your templates in a safe place for future crafting. I recommend a zip-top baggie that you keep with the rest of your papers or tucked into a bookshelf (with this book!).

Many of the templates could be customized or replaced with freehand drawing that you do yourself. Just make sure to read all the instructions for the project to make sure there is not a specific reason why the shape needs to exactly match the template I've provided. Sometimes measurements need to line up, so you'll want to use the template in those cases, and sometimes the size of a piece really does matter for the finished effect. Use your judgment and creativity, and don't be afraid to try something different!

décor

Let this be your starting point for making a magical handmade home by adding these fun décor pieces created by you!

toucan carioca

"Carioca" refers to anything from Rio de Janeiro, Brazil, which is, in my opinion, Brazil's most magical place! This colorful toucan is inspired by its vibrant colors, happy vibes, golden-orange sunsets, and everlasting happy hours to the rhythm of samba.

tip: *Try using metallic paper for some of the pieces! I used it for the light pink beak detail. For the cardboard, you can use cereal boxes or other ready-to-recycle packaging.*

Check out the ready-to-use cardstock pieces for this project on page 185!

This pullout version of the project, as well as the tracing templates on pages 169–171, will make a slightly smaller version of the toucan than is pictured in the photos. If you want to make a jumbo-sized toucan, download the digital template and increase the size by about 30%.

tools & materials

- Template (page 169)
- Cardstock in blue, hot pink, light pink, white, yellow, red, purple, green, and orange
- Cardboard, about three 9" x 11" (23 x 28 cm) pieces (or various scraps)
- Pencil
- Scissors
- Hole punch, mini if possible; mine creates ⅛" (3 mm) holes
- Glue
- Fishing line
- Ruler
- Jewelry pliers
- 2 gold jump rings, ½" (13 mm) diameter
- Yellow macrame cord
- Black marker
- Wooden dowel

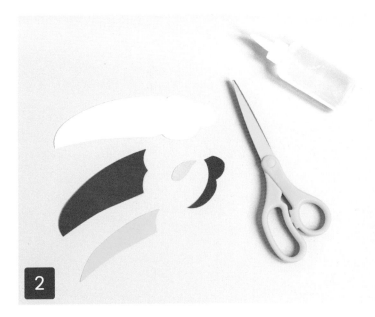

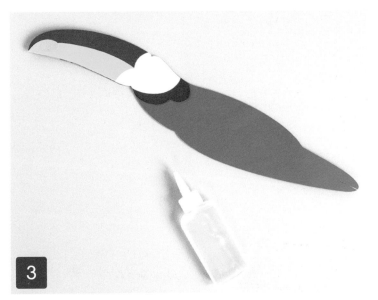

1 start the body. Using the template, trace and cut out 3 toucan bodies from cardboard and 2 toucan bodies from blue cardstock. Glue them together sandwich style, with the cardboard in the middle and the blue cardstock on the outside.

2 prepare the head. Using the template, trace and cut out 2 each of the white head, hot pink beak, yellow beak bottom, light pink beak detail, and red collar. Make sure (here and in later steps) that you are using all the template pieces on cardstock that is colored on both sides, because you will need the backside of certain pieces.

3 assemble the head. Glue each white head to the toucan body. Then, with one set of pieces at a time, glue the hot pink beak to the white head, glue the yellow beak bottom on top of that, glue the light pink beak detail in place, and then glue the red collar.

4 start the wings and tail. Using the template, trace and cut out 6 toucan wings and 2 toucan tails from cardboard and 4 toucan wings and 2 toucan tails from blue cardstock. (Only one wing set is shown here.) As you did with the body, glue the tail and each wing separately together sandwich style, with the cardboard in the middle and the blue cardstock on the outside.

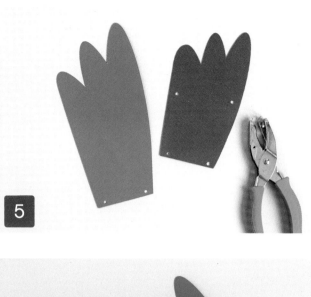

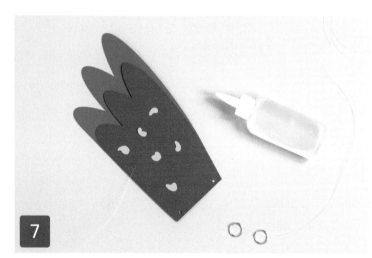

5 **prepare the pink wing tops.** Using the template, trace and cut out 2 wing tops from hot pink cardstock. Align each hot pink wing top on an assembled wing. As shown and using the template as needed for placement, use the hole punch to make four holes through each pink wing and two holes through each blue wing. The bottom holes should align.

6 **add the hanging lines.** Cut 2 pieces of fishing line 30" (77 cm) long. Work on one wing at a time. Thread one line down through one of the holes closer to the wing tip in a pink wing, then feed the line back up through the other hole next to it. Temporarily tie the ends together with plenty of slack. Then, place and align the pink wing on top of the blue wing and glue just a little of it down along the base and along the tip. You should be able to move the fishing line freely. (If you'd prefer, sometimes it's easier to use double-sided tape for this.)

7 **decorate the wings.** Glue some yellow splotches to the pink parts of the wings to add some extra magic.

8 **finish the body.** Using the template, cut out 2 purple bellies, 2 green legs, and 2 orange feet from cardstock. Glue the bellies, legs, and feet to the body. Punch a small hole in the purple belly (following the template) and a couple small holes for the jump rings along the toucan's back as shown, through all layers of cardboard and cardstock.

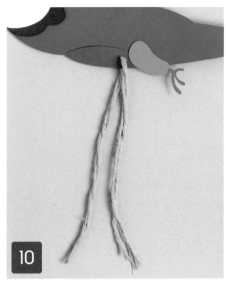

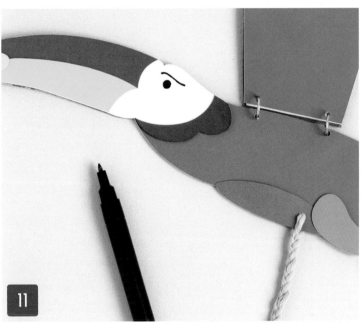

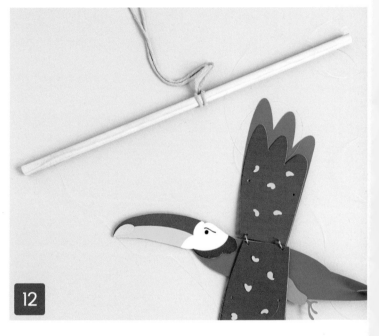

9 assemble the toucan. Using jewelry pliers, open the jump rings. Use the jump rings to assemble the toucan with one wing on either side of the body and the pink wing tops facing up.

10 add a braided detail. Cut a piece of yellow macrame cord about 16" (40 cm) long. Thread the cord through the purple belly hole so that an even amount hangs down on either side. Combine and divide the ends into three total strands, then braid about half to three-quarters of the length of the cord.

11 add final details. Using a black marker, draw the eyes on both sides of the bird's face. If you haven't already, make the straight cuts into the tail and the body, then slot the tail into place.

12 assemble the hanger. Grab the wooden dowel and tie a new length of macrame cord in the middle as shown in the step photo, or with a separate length attaching each end and forming a triangle as shown in the finished project photos. Make the hanging lengths as long as you want. To attach the toucan to the hanger, tie one fishing line length to each end of the dowel. See what length works best for you according to where you want to hang your toucan. Wiggle the bird a little bit until it is centered. It is now ready to bring all of those amazing Brazilian vibes!

leaf wreath

One of the things I miss the most about living in New York is autumn! Being able to watch the whole city turn into an orangey-golden-yellow wonderland is just so magical. Since I'm in Miami now, and everything is green almost all year long, I had to bring fall to me! This wreath offers the best of the season minus the mess of fallen leaves everywhere, so grab your pumpkin spice latte and let's say hello to fall!

tip: *You won't be able to see the cardboard once it is covered up by the leaves, so it doesn't have to be pretty! If you can't find anything sturdy enough, you can layer and glue multiple pieces together.*

tools & materials

- Template (page 178)
- Cardboard
- Ruler
- 8½" x 11" (22 x 28 cm) cardstock in your favorite color palette; I used different shades of pinks, oranges, yellows, and lilac
- Pencil
- Scissors
- Glue
- Gold glitter ribbon
- Hot glue gun

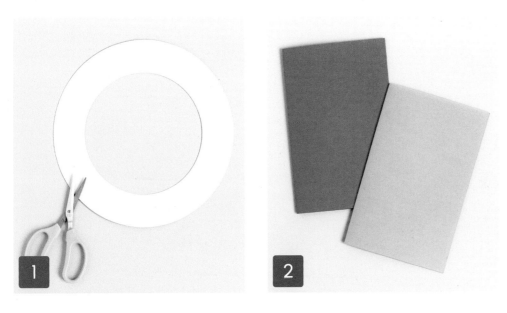

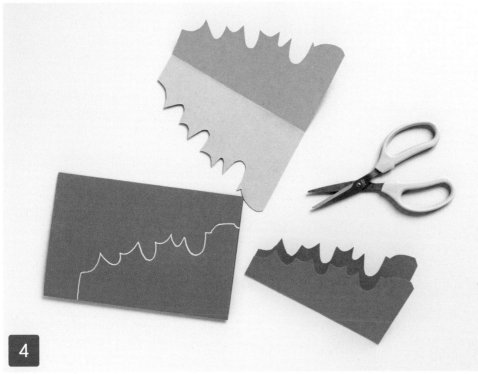

3 prepare the templates. Cut out the three leaf templates. Place one template on top of a piece of folded cardstock with the straight edge of the template aligned with the fold of the cardstock.

4 cut out the leaves. Trace around the template, then remove it and cut out the leaf by cutting through the entire piece of cardstock on the fold. You'll end up with a perfectly symmetrical full leaf. Repeat to create about 18 leaves total, mixing up the styles and colors.

1 cut the wreath base. Cut a large circle from the cardboard, then cut an inner circle inside it to create a ring. Use a large serving plate or anything round you can find in your house as a guide. The diameter of the outer circle should be about 12" (30 cm) and the width of the ring about 2½" (6.4 cm).

2 fold the cardstock. Fold the pieces of colored cardstock in half so that you have 8½" x 5½" (22 x 14 cm) pieces.

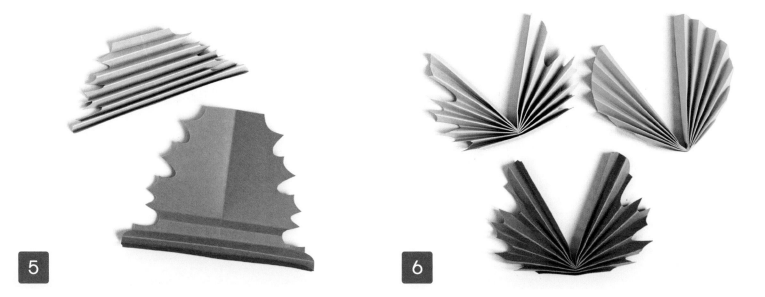

5

6

5 **accordion fold the leaves.** Accordion fold all the leaves from base to tip (not from side to side). I like them best when the folds are small and tight, but you can make them any way you like.

6 **fold the leaves in half.** Fold all the leaves in half like a fan, with the longer side of the leaf being folded inward.

7 **assemble the leaves.** Glue the longer, inner sides of each leaf together to close the "fan" and create the final leaf shape.

7

8 **add the hanger.** Cut a short piece of gold glitter ribbon about 4" (10 cm) long and fold it in half. Glue it to the back of the wreath base. If you want, you can glue a strip of leftover cardstock down over the back of the ribbon to secure it even more.

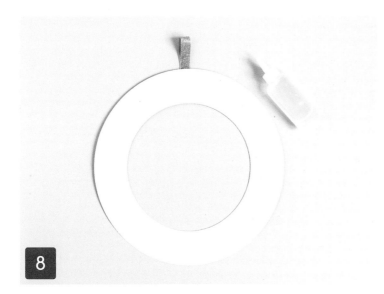

9 begin gluing. Start gluing your leaves from the bottom middle, going in one direction around the ring. You can use regular liquid glue, but hot glue makes the job much faster and more secure.

10 finish one side. Keep going until you reach the top middle of the wreath. Don't be afraid to vary how your leaves stack and layer—see how the one orange leaf here is on top of all the others?

11 finish the other side. Starting from the bottom middle again, glue leaves up the other side of the ring until they meet the other leaves at the top middle. It's time to hang and admire your wreath!

Cookies
queso

Cookies Choco
y Frambuesa

cookies naranja
y almendras

$375.-

$270

$200

palm leaves

Paper leaves are a great way to decorate your house and keep it fancy! There are many different styles you can make. I would say the palm leaf featured in the step-by-step photos is the most classic one, but I'm also sharing with you another version that I love (illustrated at the end of the project)! Put a collection of these leaves in a vase and change the color scheme according to the holiday—reds and pinks for Valentine's Day, spring pastels for Easter, oranges for Halloween, and so on!

tools & materials

- Cardstock, 19" x 25" (48 x 63 cm) or larger, one piece per leaf
- Pencil
- Scissors
- Ruler (optional)
- Glue

tip: *To make the spiky version of the leaves, see the illustrated instructions on page 43.*

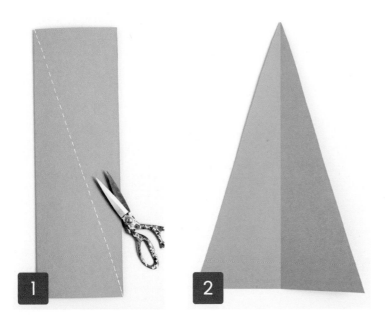

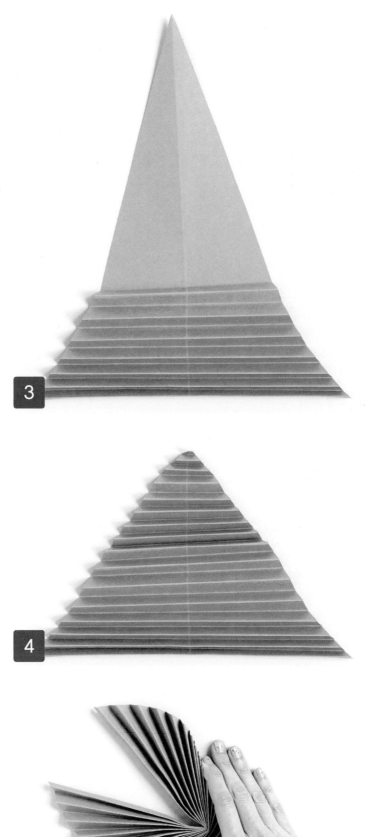

1 **fold and mark the paper.** Fold the paper in half vertically to create a long, skinny rectangle. Draw a line to divide the rectangle in half as shown.

2 **cut a triangle.** Cut along the dividing line to create one folded triangle and two basic triangles. Set the basic triangles aside for later.

3 **start folding.** Start accordion folding the paper from the bottom up. Do your best to make the folds even and straight—use a ruler if it helps. The more precise and even the folds are, the more modern and cool the finished leaf will look!

4 **finish the accordion fold.** Finish accordion folding the whole triangle, all the way to the tip.

5 **fold the leaf in half.** Rotate the folded piece so the short side is at the bottom, then pinch it in the middle to fold the leaf in half with the longer side to the inside.

6 start making the handle. Grab one of the extra triangles. Curl the tip using your scissors, just like you would to curl a gift wrapping ribbon.

7 roll the handle. Using your hands, continue curling the paper all the way down as shown and glue at the end so that you have a tight, secure tube for a handle that is thicker at the base and comes to a small point at the top.

8 flatten the handle tip. Squish the thin tip of the rolled tube and curl this flattened bit around the middle of the leaf.

9 attach the handle. Glue the flattened part of the handle to itself on the backside, making sure it is nice and snug around the leaf. You could use a hot glue gun here too.

6

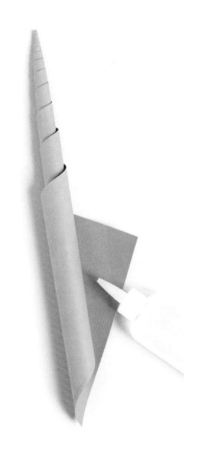

7

8

9

10 finish the palm leaf. Glue the inner leaf sides together to close the "fan" and complete the palm leaf shape.

11 make more leaves. Repeat to make more leaves to complete an aesthetic set. If you have them, try using larger pieces of paper to really make the leaves stand out. You can also mix in smaller leaves for contrast.

LET'S TRY THIS
Spiky Variation

1 Fold cardstock vertically in half. Open it up, then fold one half in half again.

2 Open it up. Cut through the second fold. The small rectangle will become your handle or "stem."

3 Rotate the cardstock so the fold line is along the bottom. Then fold it in half.

4 From the fold line up, cut the cardstock into a curved shape. The closer you get to the top, the shorter the leaves will be.

5 Open up the cardstock, then accordion fold the entire sheet from the wide base to the narrow top.

6 Fold the cardstock in half again. Cut spiky leaves as shown all the way up the open sides.

7 Open up the cardstock and accordion fold again (following the folds you already made).

8 Rotate the folded piece so the short side is at the bottom, then pinch it in the middle to fold the leaf in half with the longer side to the inside.

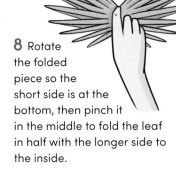

9 Using the leftover rectangle, either cut it into a triangle and roll the handle following steps 6 and 7 from the photo instructions, or simply roll the rectangle as is from one corner to create a similar effect.

10 Following steps 8 and 9 from the photo instructions, squish the tip of the handle and curl and glue it around the base of the leaf.

11 Glue the inner leaf sides together to close the "fan" and complete the palm leaf shape.

Taran!

You've created a spiky tropical leaf!

Illustrated by @letichio_ilustra

tropical
chandelier

Get tropical with this fun leaves and flowers chandelier! You can use it to decorate your room or hang it in a cute corner of your house to bring warm vibes all year long.

tip: *Depending on your paper size, you may need more or fewer sheets of paper than are listed in the Tools & Materials list to create all the elements.*

Elements List

YOU WILL CUT THE FOLLOWING FROM PAPER:

10 dark green large leaf branches

13 light green medium leaf branches

7 blue fan flower branches

8 light pink bud flower branches

20 dark pink 4-petal flowers

11 yellow 9-petal flowers

tools & materials

- Template (page 176)
- 8½" x 11" (22 x 28 cm) paper in dark green (5 sheets), light green (5 sheets), blue (3 sheets), light pink (3 sheets), dark pink (4 sheets), and yellow (2 sheets)
- Pencil
- Scissors
- Blue marker
- Glue
- Decoupage medium (optional)
- Pink glitter
- Paintbrush
- Tiny yellow pom-poms
- Needle
- Fishing line
- Ruler
- Hot glue gun (optional)
- Floral wreath hoop
- Green floral tape
- Macrame cord, ⅛" (3 mm) thickness

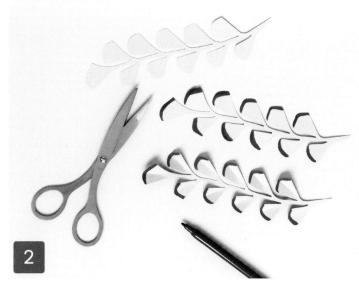

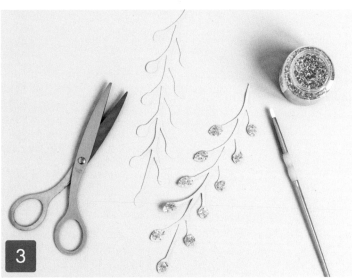

1 make the green leaves. Using the template, trace and cut out 10 dark green large leaf branches and 13 light green medium leaf branches. Fold each individual leaf on each branch in half along the center to create dimension.

2 make the blue flowers. Using the template, trace and cut out 8 blue fan flower branches. Color the bottom of each flower dark blue with a marker, then fold each individual flower on each branch in half along the center to create dimension.

3 make the light pink flowers. Using the template, trace and cut out 8 light pink bud flower branches. With a paintbrush, add some glue or decoupage medium to each individual flower. Then cover the adhesive with pink glitter. Once the adhesive is dry, add an extra layer of adhesive on top of the glitter to seal it in.

4 make the dark pink flowers. Using the template, trace and cut out 20 dark pink 4-petal flowers. With the blade of your scissors, fold each of the flower petals inward. Using a needle, thread fishing line through the center of a flower, then through a tiny yellow pom-pom. Push the pom-pom down against the flower and secure it in place with a dot of glue. Leaving some empty space between each flower, thread 4 more flowers and pom-poms onto the line. Repeat to create 4 separate strands of 5 flowers each.

5

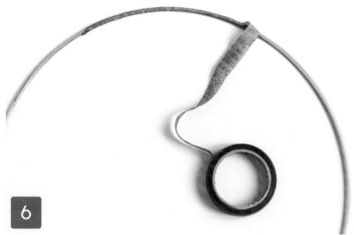

6

7

5 make the yellow flowers and prep all the strands. Using the template, trace and cut out 11 yellow 9-petal flowers. With the blade of your scissors, fold each of the flower petals inward. Finally, use your needle to make a little hole at the base of each leaf branch and the center of each yellow flower. Cut 49 lengths of fishing line about 10" (25 cm) long. Pass a separate length of fishing line through each hole with just a little bit of the line on the backside of each leaf branch and the petal side of each yellow flower. Secure each short end of fishing line with a dot of glue and let dry. If you feel comfortable with a glue gun, you can use one to work much faster—just watch your fingers!

6 cover the hoop. Cover the entire floral wreath hoop using green floral tape.

7 decide on an arrangement. Lay down your foliage on top of the hoop and come up with your favorite arrangement of colors and shapes. Set everything aside, putting one string next to the other to make it faster and easier to assemble later.

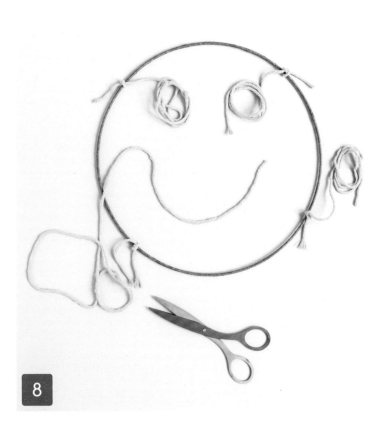

8

9

10

8 add the hanging cords. Cut 4 lengths of macrame cord and tie them to four different evenly-spaced points around the hoop. To determine how long each piece of cord should be, decide approximately how long you want the hanger to be, then add several extra inches to account for the final knot.

9 add the foliage. Tie your leaves and flowers all around the hoop. You can hang each one as low or as high as you'd like relative to the hoop—try to vary the placement, especially of the individual yellow flowers, to make the chandelier feel lush, organic, and wild.

10 finish the hanger. Tie the 4 hanging cords together, making sure the chandelier hangs in a balanced way. You can simply hang the knot from an existing hook, or you can add a hook to the knot, depending on where and how you want to hang the chandelier.

statement stars

I've always loved decorating with stars. There is something whimsical around them, and they look magical all year round. You can customize your stars by painting the paper, drawing on it, dying it, stamping it, or doing whatever you want to it! By doing so, you can create your very own version of this traditional origami craft.

tip: *I recommend listening to "Lloviendo Estrellas" by Cristian Castro while making this craft. It elevates the fun by 100%.*

tools & materials

- Paper in different colors and sizes
- Ruler (optional)
- Pencil (optional)
- Scissors
- Glue
- Hot glue gun (optional)
- Hole punch
- Gold and white twine

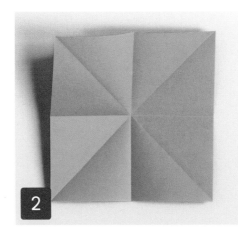
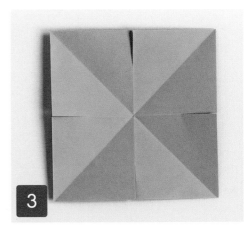

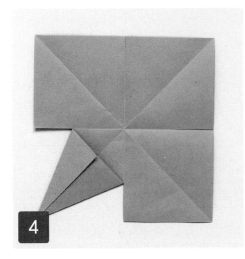

1 grab your paper. Like any traditional origami, this project starts with a simple square of paper! For the largest stars shown in the finished photos, I used 12" x 12" (31 x 31 cm) paper. For this example, I am using smaller pieces. Cut your paper down to square if it isn't already square.

2 make the initial folds. Fold the paper in half vertically, horizontally, and diagonally (in both directions) to form an X and a +.

3 make cuts. Make 4 small cuts in from the edges, one on each side, as shown—the cuts should be along the folds of the + and should go in not quite halfway to the center. Err on the side of too short—you can always snip the cut a little deeper as needed in the next step. Use a ruler and pencil if you want to be precise.

4 fold one corner. In one corner, fold the paper inward from two of the cuts to form a triangle made of two flaps as shown. The flaps should neatly align with the diagonal fold of the X in that corner. If your cut isn't quite deep enough, snip it a bit deeper. But don't worry if your cut is a little too deep—just make sure you fold the flaps in to align with the diagonal fold, not farther than that.

5 glue the corner. Pull one of the triangle flaps over to cover the other triangle flap so that the edge of the covering triangle aligns with the fold of the covered triangle. It helps to insert one or two fingers beneath the flaps as you do this. The paper will "pop up" as you pull one flap over the other, forming a three-dimensional pyramid-like point. Glue the top triangle in place on the bottom triangle. Repeat folding and gluing for the other 3 corners. You now have one 4-point star.

6 make a second star. Make another 4-point star exactly like you made the first one and in the same color and size.

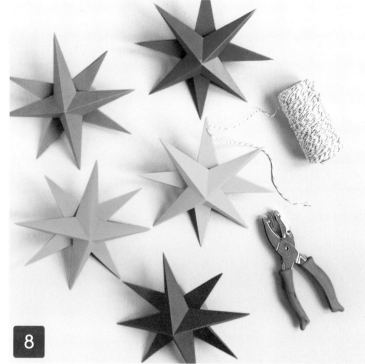

7 assemble the full star. Glue one star against the other star with the hollow in the center. You must place the glue carefully in the corners where parts of each star touch. You can use standard liquid glue or a hot glue gun.

8 add hanging twine. If you want to hang your stars, make a hole through the top point of each star using a hole punch. Then thread a length of gold and white twine through the hole. If you prefer your stars to hang from a single strand rather than a double strand, you can make a knot in one end of the twine that is bigger than the hole, and the star will stay in place.

paper chandelier

This is inspired by Polish paper chandeliers called "pajakis," which means "spiders." It's the only spider I'll ever love! It's ready to make any space a happier one. This project definitely takes a lot of tracing, cutting, folding, and wrapping, but it's worth it, so settle in.

tools & materials

- Template (page 175)
- Cardstock in shades of pink, orange, and yellow
- Pencil
- Scissors
- Hole punch
- Gold paper straws
- White and gold twine
- Ruler
- Crepe paper streamers in shades of pink and yellow
- Glue
- Scrap piece of cardboard
- Yarn in light pink
- Gold floral wreath hoop, 12" (31 cm) diameter
- Ribbon in shades of pink (optional for extra flair)
- Hot glue gun

Elements List

TOTAL PIECES NEEDED:

76 flowers, 85 straw pieces

FOR THE TOP OF THE CHANDELIER:

Cut 6 strings of white and gold twine, each 24" (60 cm) long.

All 6 strings will have 7 flowers and 8 straw pieces.

TOTAL: 42 flowers, 48 straw pieces

FOR THE BOTTOM OF THE CHANDELIER:

Cut 3 strings of white and gold twine, each 35" (90 cm) long.

2 strings will have 11 flowers and 12 straw pieces.

1 string will have 12 flowers and 13 straw pieces.

TOTAL: 34 flowers, 37 straw pieces

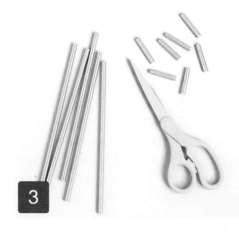

1 cut out the flowers. Using the template, trace and cut out a wide variety of flower shapes from a variety of different cardstock colors. You will need 76 flowers total. Refer to the Elements List on page 55.

2 punch holes. Punch a hole in the center of each flower.

3 cut up the straws. Cut paper straws into 4 or 5 equal pieces. You will need 85 straw pieces total.

4 string the chandelier tops and bottoms. Starting with a straw piece, thread alternating flowers and straw pieces onto lengths of gold and white twine. Refer to the Elements List on page 55 to make all of the chandelier top and bottom strings—6 top strings and 3 bottom strings. When you are done, set them all aside. Make sure you clearly separate the special, "longer" bottom string from the other two bottom strings so that you don't have to figure out which one is which later! To secure them in the meantime, you can tape the top and bottom to your table, floor, or whatever surface you are working on.

5 cut out the butterflies. Using the template, trace and cut out 6 butterflies in different colors.

6a prepare crepe paper flower pieces.

Cut 6 strips of yellow crepe paper measuring 4" (10 cm) long and 1¾" (4.5 cm) wide (the width of the streamers straight off the roll). Fringe the paper (make very thin cuts one right next to the other, about half of the width). Twist the paper into a tight flower center. Next, cut 6 strips of different shades of pink crepe paper measuring 8" (20 cm) long and 1¾" (4.5 cm) wide. Accordion fold each pink strip and, while the strip is still folded, round off the top into a semicircle. Unfold the strip to see the scalloped result.

6b assemble the crepe paper flowers.

Place some glue on the bottom corner of one end of a pink petal strip, lay the tight yellow flower center on top of it, and start rolling the pink petal strip around the yellow center. Pinch and adjust the paper as you go so that the bottom one-third of the flower becomes a tight stem and so that the petals don't all close up. Glue the flower securely closed at the end.

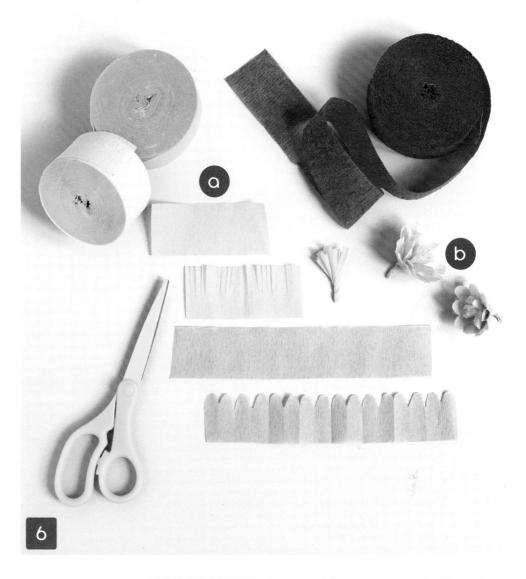

7 make the tassel.

Cut a cardboard rectangle measuring about 4" x 6" (10 x 15 cm). Start looping yarn around it, parallel to the longer side. Once it's puffy enough, thread a second, short piece of yarn underneath the entire layer of looped yarn along one edge of the cardboard and tie it in as tight a double knot as you can. Remove the yarn from the cardboard and cut the loops at the far end. Press the tassel together to give it its shape, then wrap a piece of yarn tightly around the knot end of the tassel, forming a ball shape at that end. Tie this piece of yarn off, leaving extra length to use to attach it to the chandelier later, and adjust the tassel as needed with your fingers.

8

9

10

11

8 **attach the top strings.** Tie one end of each of the 6 top strings onto the gold floral wreath hoop, spreading them out evenly.

9 **knot the top strings.** Pull the 6 strings up and tie them into a single knot, making sure the strings are balanced and leaving about 4" (10 cm) of bare twine below each knot (above the first straw piece).

10 **attach the bottom strings.** It's much easier to attach the bottom strings while the chandelier is hanging, so I suggest you hang it somewhere temporarily where you can work on it easily. As you work, don't worry about leftover string—you'll trim it all in the end. Tie each of the 2 "shorter" strings below the hoop, matching each end up with one of the top strings and the other end up with the top string directly across from the first. The flowers and straws should fall next to one another, not too tight but not too wiggly either. Then, grab the "longer" string and tie to the hoop, matching it up with the remaining top string set. This string should hang slightly below the others. You can now cut the extra string left over near all the knots!

11 **add the flowers, butterflies, ribbons, and tassel.** Refer to the finished project photos as needed. The bottom strings have been removed from this step photo for clarity.

- Put some glue on the end of each flower and glue each one right inside each top string's bottom straw piece. Push each flower up with your fingers so that it doesn't face straight down.

- Using hot glue, glue the butterflies onto the hoop, one in between each top string.

- Add various short strands of ribbon to the hoop, tying them either next to the butterflies or underneath them (before gluing the butterflies).

- Finally, tie the tassel to the bottom center of the lowest bottom string.

flower curtain

Can you imagine waking up and flowers being the first thing you see? Well, you can make that a reality with this beautiful and lush flower curtain! Making this craft just flows. There's not really a wrong way to go. Cut the flowers in bulk, stack them up, and thread them on. Before you know it, you'll have created the most magical flower garden!

tip: You don't necessarily need to use the wooden dowel to make a single flower curtain. You can tie the flower strings directly somewhere else, such as to your bedroom's curtain rod!

tools & materials

- Template (page 174)
- Tissue paper in your favorite colors
- Pencil
- Scissors
- Parchment paper
- Spray paint in gold and pink (or desired colors)
- Gold and white twine
- Measuring tape
- Needle (I recommend a large-eyed embroidery needle)
- Hot glue gun
- Wooden dowel
- Macrame cord

1 **cut the tissue paper flowers.** Depending on how dense you want your curtain to be, you will need about 25 flowers per hanging strand for . . . drumroll . . . 20 to 40 strands! That's anywhere from 500 to 1,000 flowers, so turn on some music, get into the flow, and maybe spread this project out over several days. You can cut the flowers using the template or freehanded. Save time by cutting 4 or 5 sheets stacked so you get 4 or 5 flowers at once.

2 **cut the parchment paper flowers.** Also cut some of your flowers from parchment paper. Don't worry if they curl up—they'll look great in your curtain!

3 **spray-paint some flowers.** Spray-paint your parchment paper flowers. You can lightly "splash" them with paint or paint them completely opaque. You can paint only one side or both. It's all up to you! I love using gold spray paint—it gives the flowers a glowing, magical look.

4 **thread the flowers onto the twine.** Cut 20 to 40 pieces of gold and white twine measuring about 78" (200 cm) each—make sure your strands are long enough to hang to the desired length in a door frame, with spare to tie them onto the dowel later. Grab your needle and start threading the strands of twine through the centers of the flowers. Use about 25 flowers per string, mixing the colors randomly and incorporating the spray-painted ones.

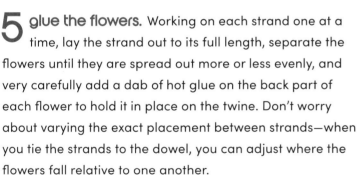

5 glue the flowers. Working on each strand one at a time, lay the strand out to its full length, separate the flowers until they are spread out more or less evenly, and very carefully add a dab of hot glue on the back part of each flower to hold it in place on the twine. Don't worry about varying the exact placement between strands—when you tie the strands to the dowel, you can adjust where the flowers fall relative to one another.

6 attach the strands to the dowel. Once you are happy with the number of flower strands you've made, tie them to a wooden dowel. You can tie them as close or as far from each other as you'd like.

7 add the hanger. Finish adding all your flower strands. Finally, tie a piece of macrame cord to the corners of your dowel and get ready to hang your masterpiece!

party

Who's ready for a fiesta? Whip up these easy projects for your next get-together. Customize the colors to suit your aesthetic or stick with my bright rainbow palette—it's your party, so craft how you want to!

cake stand

These cute little stands are just what you need to create the perfect desserts table! Make them in different sizes, heights, and colors to hold just about anything sweet you can think of. Macarons, popcorn, cupcakes, cotton candy, tiny cakes—they all deserve to be on a pedestal!

tip: *If you want to preserve your cake stands for multiple uses, put a piece of paper doily, thin cardboard, or other protective layer between your sweets and the surface of the stand to protect it from moisture and stains.*

tools & materials

- Template (page 172)
- Cardboard (about 10" x 10" [25 x 25 cm])
- Pencil
- Ruler (optional)
- Scissors (heavy-duty ones if possible)
- 2 sheets of 12" x 12" (31 x 31 cm) cardstock in your desired color
- Glue
- Paper cup
- Acrylic paint matching your cardstock color
- Paintbrush
- Double-sided tape
- Confetti
- Glitter (optional)
- Baggie of rice or other item for weight
- Hot glue gun

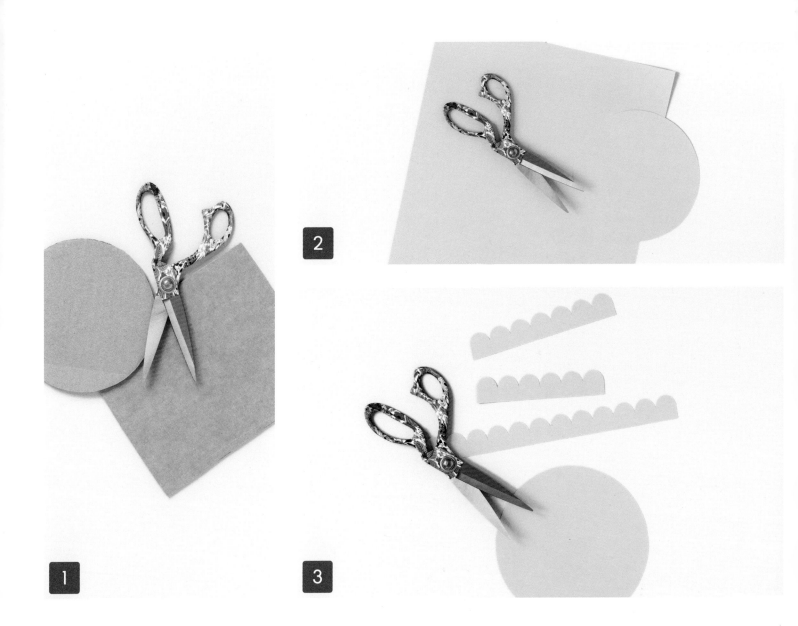

1 **cut the cardboard base.** From your cardboard, cut a circle measuring 9½" (24 cm) in diameter. You can use a large plate as a tracing template or measure the circle manually using a ruler. The size doesn't have to be exact—just make sure it's larger than the cake or other dessert you want to put on it!

2 **cut the cardstock base.** Using the cardboard circle as a template, trace and cut out a circle from colored cardstock.

3 **cut the decorative strips.** Using the template, trace and cut out strips of scalloped cardstock. Depending on your circle size, you'll need more or fewer scalloped strips. (If you go over, you can trim off the extra part and save it for a smaller cake stand!) For example, a circle with a 9½" (24 cm) diameter has a circumference of about 30" (76 cm), so you'd need about 3 full strips to go all the way around a circle of that size.

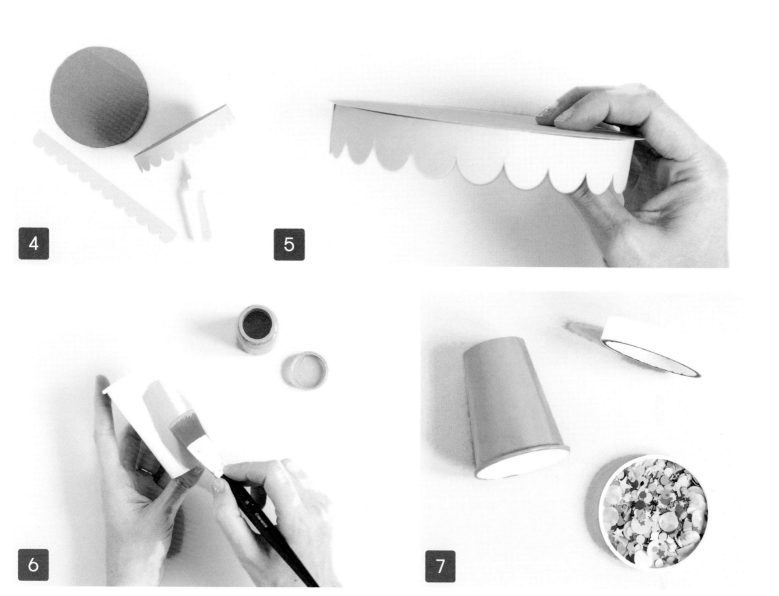

4 **glue the decorative strips.** Glue the scalloped strips around the edge of the cardboard circle.

5 **add the colored base.** Glue the colored cardstock circle to the flat side (not the scalloped side) of the cardboard circle. The scallops will hang down from the finished cake stand.

6 **paint the cup.** Grab your paper cup and start painting it. I wanted my cup color to be as close as possible to the color of the cardstock, but feel free to go as wild as you want and mix and match colors!

7 **add confetti and glitter.** Once the paint has fully dried, wrap a strip of double-sided tape around the opening of the cup, then toss confetti all over the tape. You can also manually place some confetti pieces to maximize the fill. If you want extra shimmer, add some glitter too!

8 add a weight. To add weight, sit the cup on your table as you would for drinking and place a small plastic bag inside. Start pouring rice into the bag and shaking the cup so that the rice moves all the way down and to the sides of the cup. Continue doing this until the cup is almost full, then close the bag with a knot. Cut a piece of cardboard just a tiny bit smaller than the opening of the cup. Using your glue gun, put tons of glue on the bag and push the cardboard into it. You want this to be tight. Now add some extra glue on the sides of the cardboard to seal the opening closed. Don't worry if it doesn't look good—no one will ever see it!

9 assemble the cake stand. Sit the cup with its opening side down on your workspace. Cut one or two circles (depending on their thickness) of cardboard the size of the base of the cup—you want to elevate the stand a little bit. Apply glue on all necessary surfaces to glue the cardboard to the cup base and the scalloped piece on top of the cardboard. Also add some glue around the edges of the cup base. Hold it all in place until it is dry.

confetti candles

Nothing screams "Yay, let's party!" more than this XXL confetti candle! Put it on any cake and watch your celebration escalate to the next level. This is a great way to upcycle and give a fun new twist to a boring, unused candle! I used tall, chunky candles, but you can really use any candle shape you want.

tip: *Edible glitter is best for this project, but if you don't have any, you can use real glitter. Just make sure to place it an inch or so above the base of the candle so that it doesn't go inside the cake.*

tools & materials

- Candles
- Crayons (the more colors the better!)
- Tea light candle
- Matches or lighter
- Scrap paper
- Glue (optional)
- Paintbrush (optional)
- Glitter (optional)

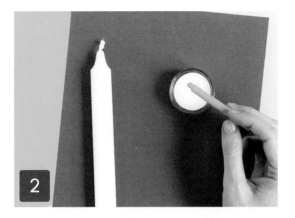

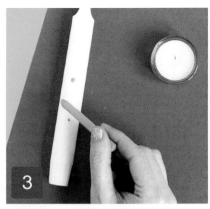

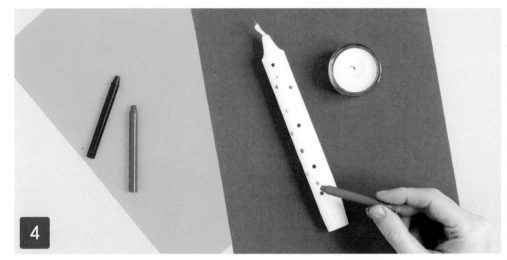

1 prep the crayons. Peel the paper off all the crayons.

2 melt a crayon. Light the tea light. Melt the tip of a crayon by holding it right up to the flame of the tea light. Melt it just enough so it is looking like it's about to start dripping.

3 drop wax dots. Carefully hover the melting crayon over the candle and let one drop of wax fall to make a dot. Repeat a few times with that color. When you're done with the color, hold it over the scrap paper for a few seconds to let the wax start to solidify, then place the crayon down on the scrap paper.

4 repeat with more colors. Repeat dropping wax dots onto the candle with as many colors as desired. Focus on just the side of the candle that is exposed in order to give the wax time to fully solidify.

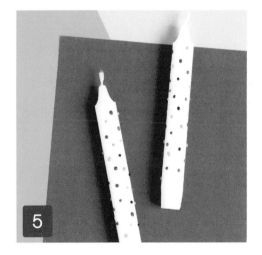

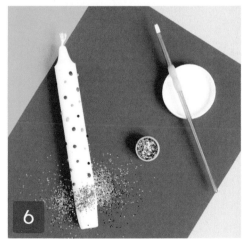

5 cover all sides. When you're done with one side and the last wax drop has fully dried, roll the candle to expose a different side, then keep adding dots until the whole candle is covered.

6 add glitter. For an extra-festive candle, you can add a band of glitter using some glue. Paint a layer of glue a few inches higher than the base of the candle and sprinkle glitter to cover it. You can hold the candle off the table to do the entire thing at once, or you can work on just one side at a time.

party crown

Everyone deserves a crown on their birthday! To be honest, I think everyone deserves a crown every day, but let's just stick to your big day for now. What I love most about this craft is that it's so easy to make, and the outcome is just adorable. As a mom of three kids, time is of the essence, so I really appreciate any pretty and simple craft that doesn't compromise on magic.

tip: *For extra pizzazz, try using sequin ribbon instead of twine for the chin strap!*

tools & materials

- Cardstock in your 6 favorite colors
- Ruler
- Pencil
- Scissors
- Double-sided tape
- Paper confetti
- Glitter
- Hole punch
- Gold and white twine

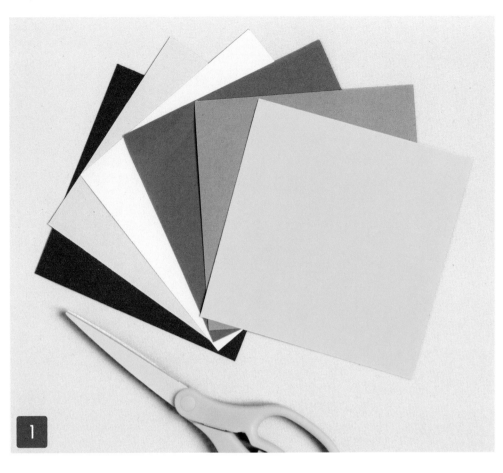

1 **cut squares.** Cut your cardstock into squares measuring 6" x 6" (15 x 15 cm). You will need 6 squares total in 6 six different colors.

2 **fold the squares.** Fold each square in half to form a triangle.

3 **nest the triangles.** Decide on the order you want the colors. Place your first color inside the second color, leaving about twenty percent of the first color showing. Repeat to nest all the triangles in a row.

4 curve the crown. Using both hands, grab each corner of the triangle row. Gently and carefully fold the row into a circle, doing your best not to shift how much of each triangle is exposed.

5 close the crown. To close the crown, place the last triangle on the right side into the pocket of the first triangle on the left side. Adjust all the triangles as needed to even them out.

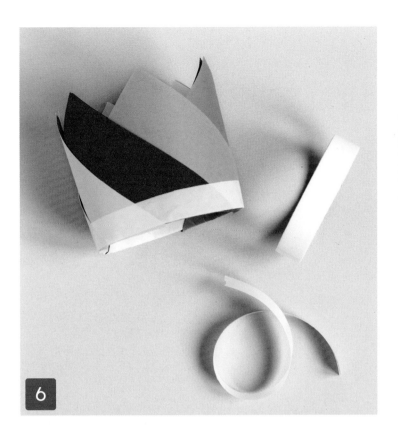

9

10

6 **add tape.** Wrap a strip of double-sided tape around the entire base of the crown.

7 **add confetti.** Toss confetti all over it! Use your fingers to press the confetti securely into the tape. Rotate the crown so you cover the tape with confetti all the way around.

8 **add glitter.** Sprinkle glitter all over the tape to fill in any gaps and add some sparkle.

9 **add holes.** Use a hole punch to make two holes on opposite sides of the crown, through the layer of confetti and tape.

10 **add the chin strap.** Tie a strand of gold and white twine on each side, using pieces that are long enough to be brought together and tied under your chin.

party poppers

This craft is awesome because you can finally put to good use all those paper rolls you've been saving all year! These confetti poppers are makeable in less than five minutes and are guaranteed to bring fun and happiness to any celebration. They're also a great way to dig into your scrap stash and use up old balloons and pieces of cardstock. Make one for every person attending your party, and make them in a rainbow of colors or coordinating with your party décor.

tools & materials

- Paper rolls
- Cardstock (this is a great craft for scraps!)
- Pencil
- Scissors
- Glue
- Balloons
- Double-sided tape
- Paper confetti
- Other confetti or glitter

tip: *Keep a jar of confetti at the ready during your party so that people can refill their party poppers and use them again!*

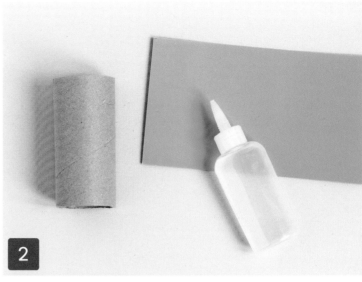

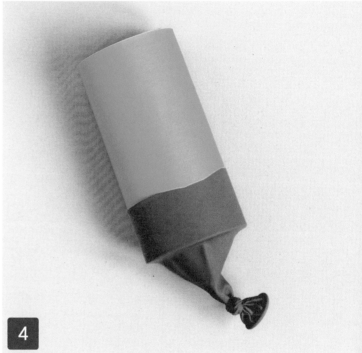

1 cut a rectangle. Use a paper roll and a pencil to measure and cut a rectangle of cardstock to wrap around the paper roll and completely cover it.

2 wrap the paper roll. Glue the cardstock rectangle to the paper roll. Make sure you hold it in place long enough to ensure the paper sticks and doesn't unroll itself as it dries.

3 prep the balloon. Tie a knot to close the balloon (without blowing it up!). Cut off a small part of the top of the balloon. Start by cutting off just a very small bit and checking the fit in step 4—you can always cut off more, but not less.

4 add the balloon. Put the balloon onto one end of the paper roll. Make sure it's snug. If it's too loose, your popper might fall apart, so if that is the case, start again with a fresh balloon.

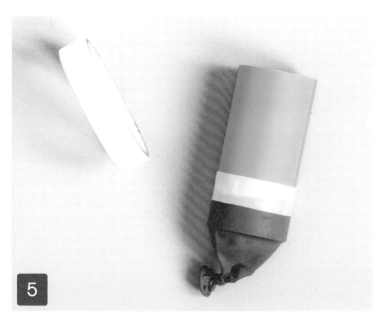

5 **add double-sided tape.** Place double-sided tape all around the area where the balloon and the paper roll meet. This will help hold the balloon in place and also allow you to decorate it.

6 **decorate with confetti.** Here's the fun part: toss confetti all over it! Use your fingers to press the confetti securely into the tape. Cover it all the way around.

7 **make more poppers.** Repeat to make several poppers in different colors. You can personalize these poppers in so many different ways! Try using printed photos to honor a birthday, team colors for the big game, and so on!

8 **fill and use the poppers.** To use a popper, first dump some confetti into the open end and jiggle it to get it to settle down in the balloon. Aim the popper (not at anyone's face!), pull the balloon knot, and let it go to launch the blast of color!

butterfly crown

Butterflies on your head? Yes, please! Make this super-easy headband and get ready to celebrate just about anything. You can color the shapes inside the butterfly wings, or you can cut them out for a more intricate effect.

tip: *If you want to ensure the crown stays in place on your head, test fit it and then use hot glue to adhere a bobby pin or barrette to the underside where it won't be visible while you're wearing the crown.*

tools & materials

- Template (page 175)
- Cardstock in 8 colors (this is a good project for using up scraps!)
- Pencil
- Scissors
- Markers in 8 colors
- Glue

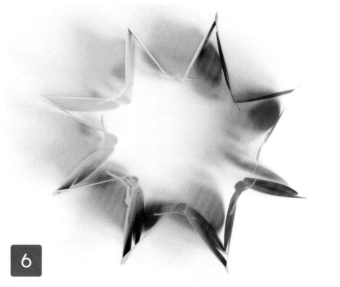

1 cut out the butterflies. Using the template, trace and cut out 8 butterflies from cardstock, each in a different color. Using 8 butterflies will give the crown enough extra to "stretch" so one size fits almost all!

2 add color. Color in the shapes on each butterfly using a color that matches the paper. You can freehand this coloring or cut holes in the template and use it to trace the shapes on each butterfly.

3 add detail. Finish coloring all the butterflies. Include dots along the wing edges and don't forget to fill in the antennae and bodies.

4 fold the wing tips. Fold the tip of each top wing inward.

5 start assembling the crown. Arrange the butterflies in your desired color order. Fold each wing up from the body, leaving the body flat. Then, one by one, glue the folded tip of one butterfly wing to the folded tip of the next butterfly wing.

6 finish assembling. Glue the last butterfly wing tip to the very first butterfly wing tip. Your crown will look like this once you've glued it all!

flowers

"There are always flowers for those who want to see them."
—*Henri Matisse*

Grab some crepe paper, cardstock, and paint, and let's create a magical garden!

cherry blossoms

I must have flowers, always and always, said the great Monet, and I couldn't be more in agreement! Flowers just make life happier, and even though nature's versions are stunning, there's also a little something special about creating them with your own two hands.

Cherry blossoms in particular are truly magical. I dream of traveling to Japan to see them in full bloom. In the meantime, botanical gardens will have to do. But you'll be surprised how easy they are to make and how real they can look when they are on a branch!

tip: *Any salvaged branch from your yard or a park will do for this project (just make sure it has already fallen). For my final version, I got a real cherry blossom branch—with flowers blooming on it! So I decided to add my paper flowers to the real thing and mix and match a little. In time, the real flowers will fall, but the paper ones will stay forever, making this a beautiful décor piece filled with happy memories.*

tools & materials

- Template (page 174)
- Italian crepe paper (180-gram weight) in pink and yellow
- Scissors
- Ruler
- Bordeaux marker or colored pencil
- Pencil
- Tree branch (real or artificial)
- Rag or paper towel (optional)
- Hot glue gun

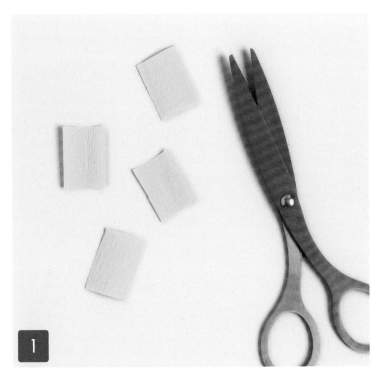

1 cut yellow pistils. Cut small rectangles of yellow crepe paper that measure about 1¼" x ¾" (3 x 2 cm) each. Cut one for every individual blossom you'd like to make. Make sure the grain of the paper is vertical. This will be the center of your flower—the pistils.

2 color the pistils. Using your Bordeaux marker or colored pencil, color about 85 percent of each rectangle of yellow crepe paper, leaving a thin line of yellow untouched at the top. Next, make thin cuts down from the yellow side almost all the way to the base, one right next to the other. Twirl each fringed rectangle to roll it together into a pistil shape as shown.

3 **cut and color the petals.** Cut small rectangles of pink crepe paper that measure about 2" x 1¼" (5 x 3 cm) each. Make sure the grain of the paper is vertical. Using the template, trace and cut out the petal shape. Make 5 petals per flower. Color the base of each petal using the Bordeaux marker or colored pencil, but not as densely as you colored the yellow paper.

4 **stretch the petals.** Using both fingers, gently stretch the paper out in the middle so that the petals widen. The crepe paper should hold its expanded shape.

5 **assemble the blossoms.** Start gluing the pink petals around the yellow pistils, gluing them to the base of each pistil. Slightly overlap each petal as you go around. Use 5 petals per flower. Make as many flowers as you'd like. For me, the more, the merrier!

6 prepare the branch. Grab your branch and clean it of any dust and dirt if needed using a rag or paper towel. Snap or cut off any bits that you don't want in the final shape.

7 glue on the blossoms. Start gluing the flowers to the branch. I recommend using hot glue for a much faster crafting time, but you can also use regular glue and hold each blossom in place until the glue dries.

giant flower

I first started making these giant paper flowers for spring. But as seasons went by and the flowers disappeared, I started to miss them! So I began making them to fill up my art studio with their happiness all year round. Try making them in hues of pinks, oranges, purples, or blues! Mix and match papers to create an infinite garden of magical flowers. The blue, white, and grayish final version I made may look like a regular flower, but the truth is, it's an Argentine escarapela in disguise! Every national holiday, escarapelas are worn to celebrate our union and love for our country. We wear them proudly on the left side of our chest (where the heart is). This XL version of it is just a big reminder of how much I love my home country.

tip: *Tissue paper is typically sold in sheets with a rectangle shape. I oriented each rectangle horizontally and measured its height. These heights are the measurements included in the list to the right. With all the paper oriented horizontally, you might see that the rectangles differ a little bit in length. That's totally okay—if it's not a huge difference, it won't be noticeable in the final flower!*

tools & materials

- Tissue paper in white, gold, and 4 shades of blue (see sizes and quantities below)
- Measuring tape
- Scissors
- Green florist wire
- Wire cutters or old scissors
- Glue

Elements List

YOU WILL NEED TISSUE PAPER SHEETS IN THESE COLORS AND SIZES:

3 light blue,
measuring about 20" (50 cm)

3 grayish blue,
measuring about 16" (40 cm)

3 washed blue,
measuring about 15" (37 cm)

3 white,
measuring about 13" (32 cm)

2 turquoise,
measuring about 12" (29 cm)

2 white,
measuring about 8" (21 cm)

1 gold strip, measuring about
8" x 20" (21 x 50 cm) long

1

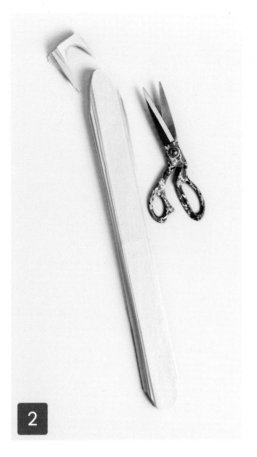

2

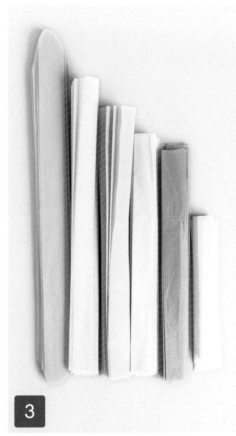

3

1 accordion fold the light blue sheets. Grab the 3 light blue sheets of tissue paper (refer to the list on page 101), put them one on top of the other, and accordion fold them vertically. You can fold them with each strip being as thick or as thin as you'd like. I usually fold mine with strips of around 2¾" (7 cm) thick. Don't worry if your final folded version isn't the same as mine.

2 round the ends. Cut both ends of the folded stack into half-circles.

3 repeat with the other colors. Repeat this folding and shaping process with all the other papers in the sets listed on page 101 (everything but the gold strip). Separate the paper by color and accordion fold each set separately.

4 stack the colors. Unfold all the sets and stack them together in the following order from bottom to top, largest to smallest, with one end of each aligned: 3 light blue, 3 grayish blue, 3 washed blue, 3 white, 2 turquoise, 2 white.

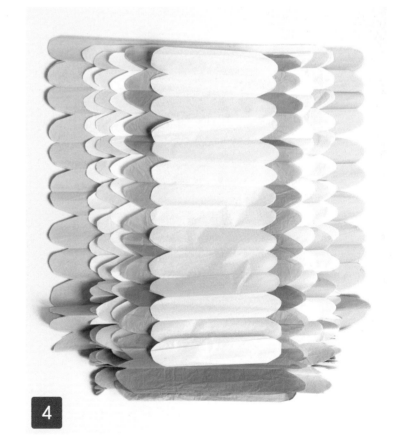

4

5 fold the set. Fold the entire stacked set into one big accordion.

6 pinch. Pinch in the middle of the folded set.

7 add wire. Cut a piece of florist wire about 8" (20 cm) long. Fold it in half and wrap it around the pinched middle of the paper stack. Flip the stacked paper around to the backside (where the bottom layer of light blue paper is) and twist the wire tightly with the twist sitting on the backside (rather than to the right or left side). Fold down the twisted wire so that no one gets poked later.

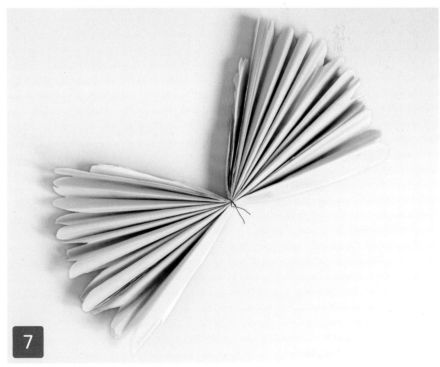

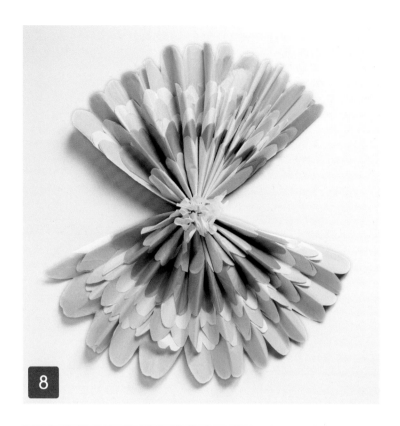

8

9

10

11

12

8 start lifting petals. Flip the stacked paper back around to the front side. Start pulling up the separate layers of paper to turn them into petals. Pull them up one sheet at a time (not one stack of color at a time), starting with the first white layer on one side of the tie, then on the other.

9 continue lifting petals. Keep going with more colors and layers. Tissue paper is very delicate, so be mindful of your super strength when doing so.

10 finish the last petals. When you reach the last layer, it may be easier to lift the flower up and turn it slightly to the side to pull up the final light blue petals.

11 make the gold strip. Cut a strip of gold tissue paper about 8" x 20" (21 x 50 cm) long. Fold it in half so that it measures about 4" x 20" (10 x 50 cm) long. Make short little cuts to fringe the paper on the folded side all the way along the length.

12 shape the center. Roll the fringed gold strip into a bundle and secure it closed with a little bit of glue.

13 add the center. Use your fingers to gently make some space in between the white petals in the center of the flower so the gold piece can fit in neatly. Put some glue on the bottom of the gold piece and glue it into the center.

13

forever plant

Even though I'm one million percent a city girl, I have a crazy obsession with plants. I love them so much—but I'm just not sure that they love me back! After many failed and sad attempts to have an indoor garden in my house, I decided that I needed to get creative. So, I picked a couple of very low-maintenance real plants (like cactuses) and mixed them with handmade paper plants to create my magical, thriving indoor garden! It's all the happiness with none of the heartbreak—the best way to go!

tools & materials

- Template (page 179)
- Cardstock in light pink and dark pink, about 6 sheets per color
- Pencil
- Scissors
- Acrylic paint in dark green and white
- Paintbrush
- White acrylic marker
- Ruler
- Green florist wire
- Green floral tape
- Wire cutters or old scissors
- Glue

tip: *The cool thing about making your own plants is that you don't necessarily have to stick to real plant shapes or colors—so go crazy! Blow up the scale, make purple and blue leaves, add gold spots or even confetti dots . . . there's no wrong way to go!*

1

2

1 **cut the leaves.** Using the template, trace and cut out leaves from light pink and dark pink cardstock. Cut 5 large leaves, 6 medium leaves, and 3 small leaves from both colors of cardstock so that you have a total of 10 large, 12 medium, and 6 small leaves at the end. Each finished leaf is assembled using one of each color of leaf.

2 **paint the leaves.** Paint leaf details on all the light pink leaves. I like to start in the middle and work outward with gentle brushstrokes. Start painting with the dark green. Then, create a lighter green tone by adding white to the dark green paint. Add strokes of the light green paint over the dark green. Have fun while you paint, experiment with what you like best, and make each leaf different and unique!

3 **add details to the leaves.** Once the green paint has dried, add extra touches using a white acrylic marker or white acrylic paint. Add a central vein down the middle of each leaf. (In the botanical world, this is called the midrib.)

3

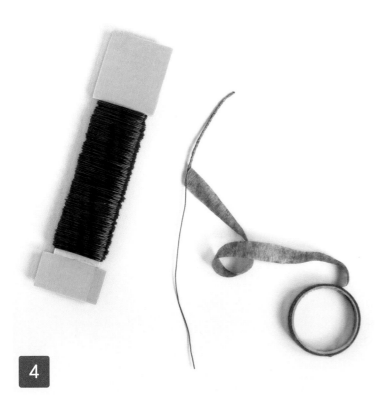

4 **prepare the leaf stems.** Cut a piece of green floral wire for each leaf to be assembled. The large leaves will need a 12" (30 cm) piece of wire and the medium and small leaves will need an 8" (20 cm) piece of wire. Wrap each piece of wire with green floral tape to completely cover it.

5 **assemble the leaves.** Glue a wrapped wire to the back (unpainted) side of a light pink leaf with at least a couple inches extending down from the stem of the leaf. Glue a dark pink leaf of the same size on top of it to sandwich and cover the wire. Make sure to glue all the borders well. Repeat until you have assembled all the leaves.

6 **make the main stem.** For the main plant stem, cut 5 pieces of green floral wire about 16" (40 cm) long. You can also fold the wire in one piece instead of cutting 5 pieces—to do this, measure 16" (40 cm) of the wire and then fold it back and forth 5 times using the 16" (40 cm) as a "ruler." This measurement is approximate; it doesn't have to be exact! Wrap all the wire together with green floral tape to completely cover it. At one end, add extra layers of tape across and around the tip to create a little bud.

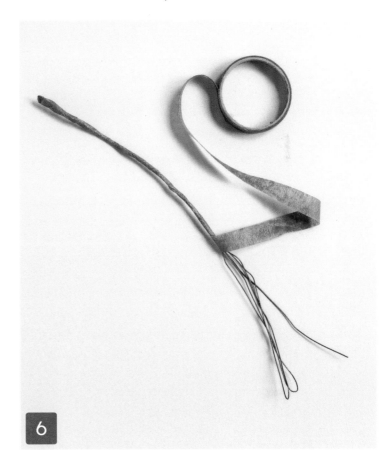

7 **begin attaching leaves.** Now it's time to attach the leaves to the main stem using the floral tape. Start near the top (bud end) of the main stem with the smaller leaves. The smaller leaves should be at the top and center and the bigger leaves at the bottom and exterior.

8 **add the rest of the leaves.** Keep adding leaves down the stem, increasing in size. You can change your mind and peel off the floral tape as you go if you want to adjust the placement of a leaf as you're working. At the end, the plant will look full and happy. You should have some stem left over at the bottom, which you can stick into a pot or flower vase, using pebbles or other filler to make the plant stand upright. Voilà! You can now call yourself a PLANT LADY!

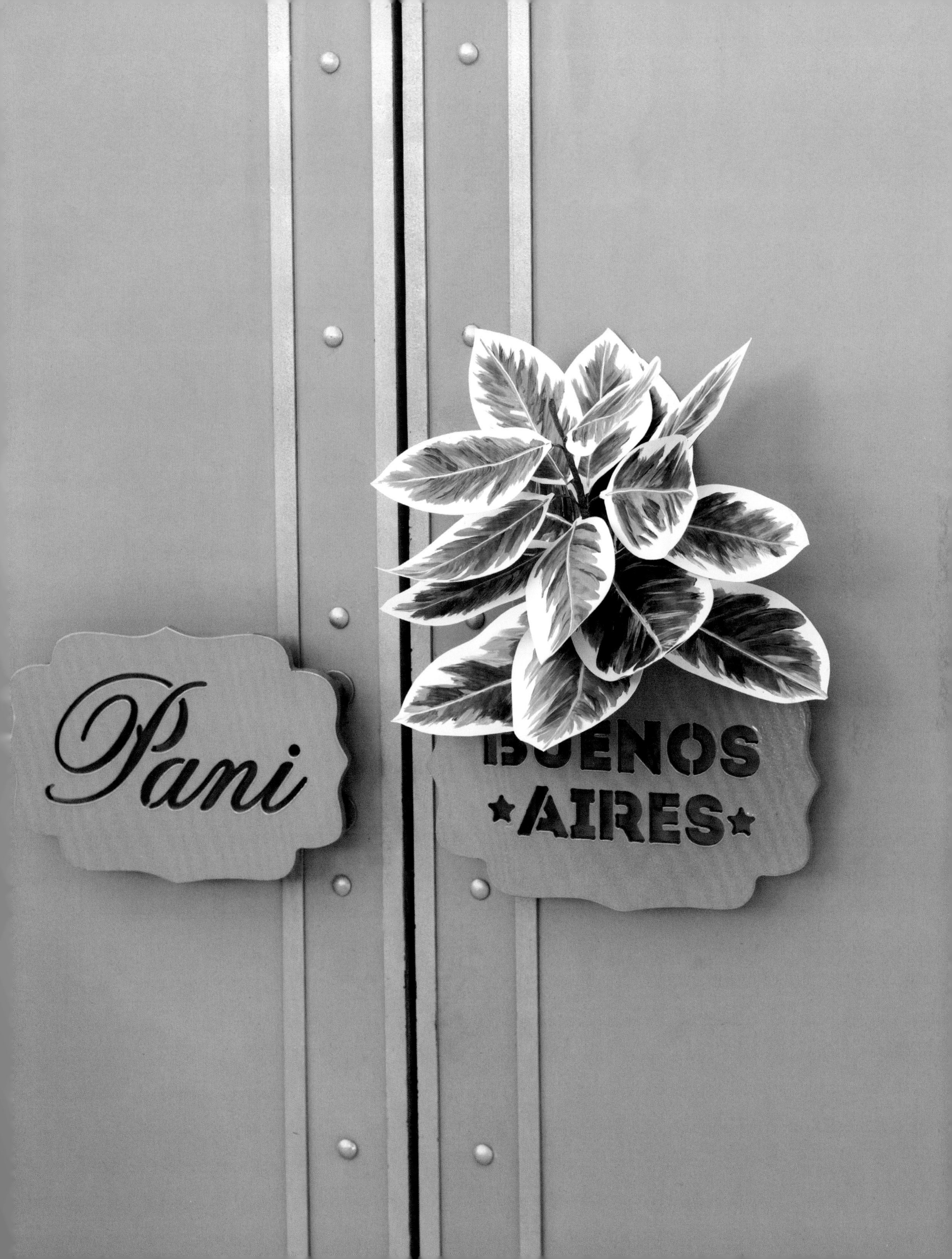
Pani
BUENOS
AIRES

poppies

Poppies are such joyful flowers! I love how their petals open up so freely and wildly. They come in an array of colors—pinks, yellows, oranges . . . so dreamy! I hope you enjoy crafting my happy version of this stunning flower!

tip: *It's always fun to mix and match paper flowers with real ones! If you decide you'd like to try this option, you can skip the green floral tape at the bottom of the wire—that way, it won't get ruined with water! Just cover the visible upper part of the flower with tape, and they are ready!*

tools & materials

- Template (page 174)
- Green florist wire
- Ruler
- Paper towel, napkin, or tissue
- Glue
- Green floral tape
- Italian crepe paper (180-gram weight) in yellow, dark yellow, and blush
- Scissors
- Pencil
- Blush chalk

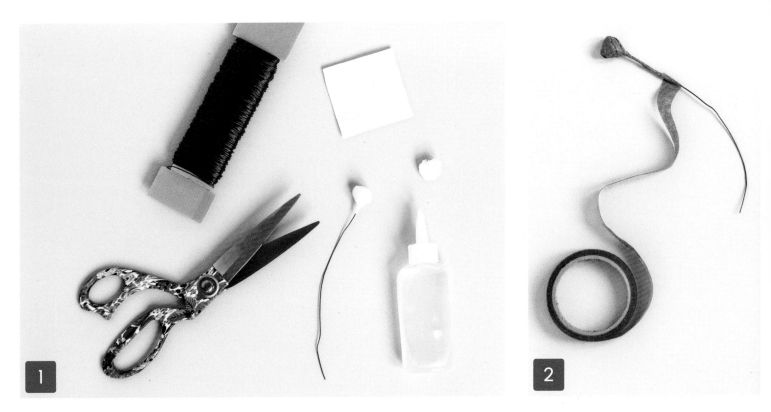

1 prepare the bud. Cut a piece of floral wire about 8"
(20 cm) long. Cut a small square of paper towel, napkin,
or tissue and roll it into a ball. Glue it to one end of the wire.

2 cover the bud. Cover the paper ball and the entire
wire using floral tape.

3 make one yellow strip. Cut a narrow strip of yellow
crepe paper with the grain running perpendicular to
the length. It can be a little shorter than the wire. Stretch
it out and twist it so it becomes similar to a strand of
embroidery thread.

4 wrap the bud. Using a little bit of glue, wrap the
yellow strand around the bud to make a star shape.
Start by placing the strand along the stem of the flower up
over the bud. Pinch it in and wrap it at the base of the bud
and then wrap it back up over the bud. Repeat until you
have an 8-point star.

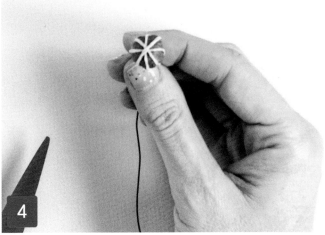

5 **secure the wrapping.** Use floral tape to cover and adhere both ends of the yellow strand to the stem.

6 **cut flower petals.** Using the template, trace and cut out 8 flower petals from the pink crepe paper. Make sure the grain is running from base to tip.

7 **color the petals.** Color the base of each of the petals using blush chalk.

8 **fold and twist the petals.** Accordion fold each petal, twist the whole thing, and then open it back up.

9

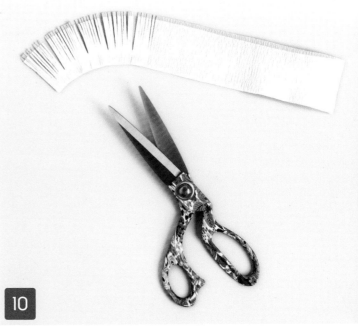

10

11

9 shape the petals. Press the center of each petal with your thumbs and stretch the paper outward a little with your fingers to create a realistic petal. Repeat for all the petals.

10 make the pistils. Cut 2 strips of light yellow crepe paper measuring 1¾" (4.5 cm) tall and 4" (10 cm) long and 1 strip of dark yellow crepe paper measuring 2" (5 cm) tall and 4" (10 cm) long. Stretch them out as much as you can (they will approximately double in length) and glue them together with the dark yellow in the middle so that a thin strip of dark yellow is visible along the top edge of the sandwich. Once it dries, fringe the paper with deep, closely-spaced cuts, cutting in from the dark yellow side.

11 attach the pistils. Put some glue along the base of the fringed strip and twirl it around the bud. Make sure the end is secured with glue after you finish wrapping it.

12 **attach the petals.** Start gluing the petals around the flower center one by one, slightly overlapping each one. Use 8 petals per flower.

13 **wrap the base.** Using floral tape, cover the base of the flower and continue wrapping the tape all the way down to the end of the stem. Your flower is looking good!

sun flowers

Having flowers around makes me so happy! I love all types of flowers, but there's something magical about sunflowers. They are always looking for sunshine, kind of like how we should always look for the positive side of life. These everlasting paper versions are guaranteed to make you smile every time you see them!

tip: *My crafty friend Delfi has taught me the magic of working in series! This is the best way to make a whole bunch of sunflowers in speedy mode. Cut 6 strips of light brown paper, 6 strips of dark brown paper, and 6 strips of black paper, and you'll be making the center of 6 flowers so much faster! Repeat the same strategy for all the other elements of the flower, and, before you know it, you'll feel like you could open a flower shop!*

tools & materials

- Template (page 179)
- Italian crepe paper (180-gram weight) in yellow, black, light brown, dark brown, and green
- Pencil
- Scissors
- Orange colored pencil
- Ruler
- Aluminum foil
- Green floral tape
- Glue

1 cut and color the petals. Using the template, trace and cut out about 30 petals per sunflower from yellow crepe paper. Make sure the grain is running from base to tip. Then color the bottom of each petal with an orange pencil to give the petals some depth.

2 shape the petals. Using both fingers, stretch out the middle of each petal and pinch the bottom.

3 prep the black flower center. Cut a strip of black crepe paper measuring 3" x 24" (8 x 60 cm) with the grain running perpendicular to the length. Stretch it out as much as you can (it will approximately double in length). Fold it in half to create a narrow strip. Along the folded side, cut shallow fringe (about half of the width of the strip) using relatively widely-spaced cuts.

4 prep the brown flower center. Cut 1 strip of dark brown crepe paper measuring 2½" x 30" (6 x 75 cm) with the grain running perpendicular to the length. Stretch it out as much as you can (it will approximately double in length). Repeat with 1 strip of light brown crepe paper that is 2" x 15" (5 x 37 cm). Fold the strips of paper horizontally (like an accordion) once or twice to allow yourself to cut through more layers faster. Using sharp scissors, cut fringe (about half of the width of the strip) using closely-spaced cuts.

5 make the stem. Use aluminum foil to make a long flower stem—simply roll and squeeze a strip of foil into the desired shape and thickness. Then cover it with floral tape. I made my stem about 10½" (27 cm) long.

6 attach the black strip. Glue the bottom of one end of the black strip to the top of the flower stem and start twirling the paper around the stem, adding glue as you go to secure the whole thing.

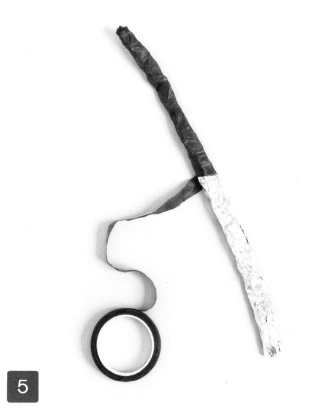

5

6

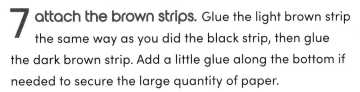

7 attach the brown strips. Glue the light brown strip the same way as you did the black strip, then glue the dark brown strip. Add a little glue along the bottom if needed to secure the large quantity of paper.

8 add petals. Start gluing the petals around the brown flower center, placing them on the brown fringe. One method is to glue a row all the way around with each petal next to each other, then go around a second row with the petals staggered to fall between each of the petals in the first row. Repeat until you've used up all your petals or are happy with the result. You can also glue the petals more randomly, as shown here, rather than in rows.

9 make the leaves. Using the template, trace and cut out about 6 leaves from green crepe paper. Make sure the grain is running from base to tip. Stretch out the middle of each leaf using both fingers. You can use a light green colored pencil to add detail to the leaves if you'd like!

10 attach the leaves. Start gluing the leaves around the base of the sunflower. Overlap the leaves until you have covered the whole base of the flower. Once you are done gluing the leaves, add another layer of floral tape to unify the flower base and the stem.

style

These crafty accessories are
ready to bring you joy and make
your days oh là là très chic!

confetti purse

By this point you've probably realized how much I love confetti, right? I carry confetti with me wherever I go. You never know when you may need it—and confetti is ALWAYS the answer! So, I thought, why not a confetti purse? To carry more confetti, of course.

tip: *How fun would this purse be if you made it with holographic or iridescent contact paper? Oooh, the possibilities!*

tools & materials

- Transparent self-adhesive contact paper
- Pencil
- Measuring tape
- Scissors
- Confetti
- Gold glitter
- Gold vinyl (adhesive or nonadhesive)
- 2 strong round magnets, $^{11}/_{16}$" (18 mm) diameter
- Superglue
- Hole punch
- Gold ribbon
- Gold metal chain purse strap (with clip/ring on each end for attaching)

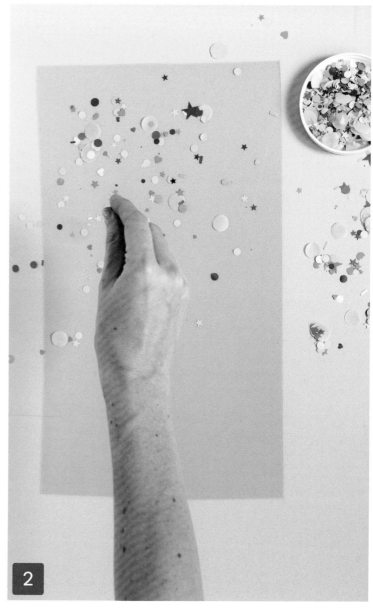

1 **cut the contact paper.** Cut 2 rectangles of clear contact paper measuring 19" x 10" (48 x 25 cm) each.

2 **add confetti and glitter.** On the sticky side of one sheet, toss confetti all over. Then add gold glitter for extra sparkle!

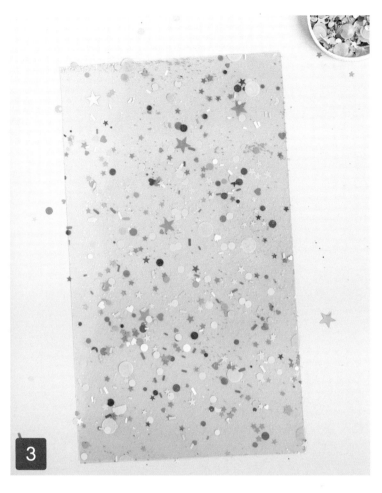

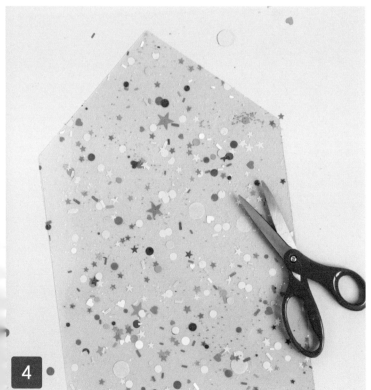

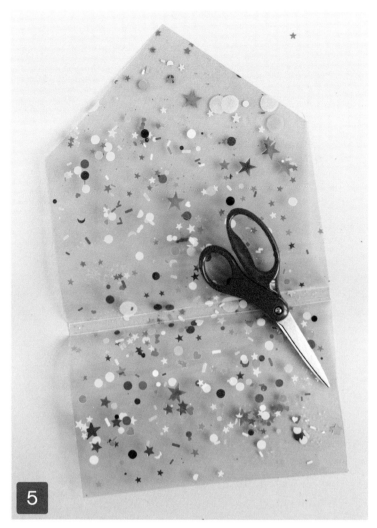

3 combine the sheets. Stick the two sheets together, one on top of the other and perfectly aligned, with both sticky sides in, effectively sandwiching the confetti layer you added to the first sheet.

4 cut the flap. With the rectangle oriented vertically, measure 4¾" (12 cm) down from the top on both the left side and the right side and mark with a pencil. Then measure 5" (12.5 cm) in from the left on the top. Cut from the middle mark to each left and right mark, forming a triangle.

5 fold the base. Fold the rectangle under at 11¾" (30 cm) from the top (measuring from the point of the triangle) and then under again ⅜" or ½" (1 or 1.3 cm) farther, creating a ⅜" or ½" (1 or 1.3 cm) base. Open it up and you'll start to see the purse shape!

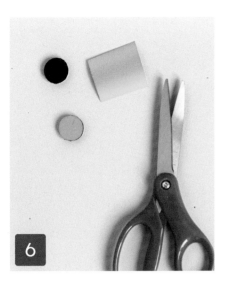

6 cover the magnets. Cut two gold vinyl circles to cover one side of each magnet. If you do not have adhesive vinyl, use superglue.

7 attach the magnets. Using superglue, glue one magnet to the top of the triangle flap, placing it as desired (I placed mine slightly over the edge) and with the gold vinyl side to the outside of the flap. Close the flap as if closing the purse, and mark where the magnet hits on the purse body. Glue the other magnet in place on the purse body on the inside of the purse, not on the outside, so it's more secure, applying the glue on top of the gold vinyl.

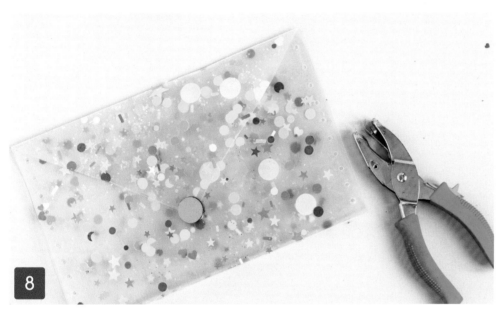

8 punch holes. Close the purse. Using a hole punch, make holes all the way up each side of the purse, stopping before the edges of the flap. The number of holes and amount of space between each hole will vary according to the size of holes your hole punch makes. Mine makes very small ⅛" (3 mm) holes, so I was able to fit 10 holes on each side. You may have to make fewer or more holes. You must make an even number of holes, not an odd number of holes.

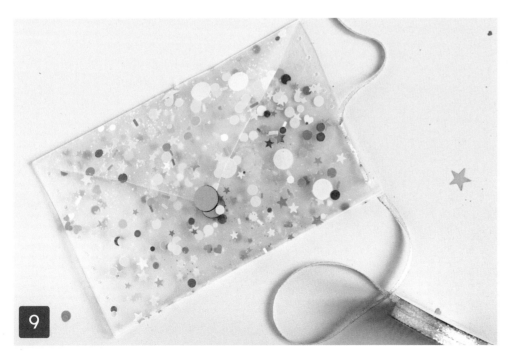

9 weave in ribbon. Starting from the back (non-flap) side, insert gold ribbon up through the bottom hole and weave it in and out of the holes until you reach the top hole.

10

10 glue the ribbon. At the top
hole, pass the ribbon down
through to the backside, pull and
adjust the ribbon until both ends
overlap a little on the backside, and
glue the ribbons to each other and to
the purse. Repeat this weaving and
gluing operation on the other side of
the purse. Make sure you use powerful
glue here. You could also tie the ribbon
together with a knot at the bottom,
similar to what is done in the Upcycled
Wallet project.

11 add the strap. Attach the metal
purse strap chain through each of
the top holes of the purse. Depending
on the size of the chain or chain clip,
you may need to make this top hole
a little bit bigger. You are ready to
rumble!

11

flower shoes

Take flowers with you everywhere you go with these cute little flower shoes! They are very easy to make and are guaranteed to elevate your outfit the minute you put them on, bringing pep to your step and brightening the world around you.

tip: *Glue bigger pom-poms to the end of your laces for an extra-fun detail!*

tools & materials

- Template (page 173)
- White cotton canvas sneakers
- Painter's tape
- 8½" x 11" (22 x 28 cm) sheet of printable vinyl sticker paper
- Scissors
- Scrap newspapers, magazines, napkins, or paper towels
- Spray paint in your favorite color (I used pink)
- White fabric paint (optional)
- Paintbrush (optional)
- Yellow mini pom-poms
- Glue (fabric glue if possible)
- Hot glue gun (optional) (with fabric glue sticks if possible)
- Yellow standard-size pom-poms (optional)

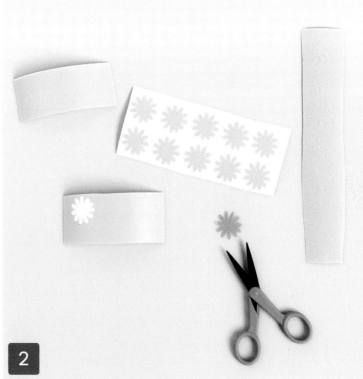

1 **prep the shoes.** Mask the soles of the shoes using painter's tape. Carefully press down the tape to protect everywhere you want to keep the paint off. Remove the laces.

2 **prep the stickers.** Make a copy or scan of the flower template. Use it to print out the flowers directly on vinyl sticker paper. You could also cut out a template flower and trace it directly onto vinyl sticker paper instead of printing. Cut out each sticker. If you have an electronic cutting machine, you can do this whole process even quicker!

3 **sticker the shoes.** Peel each sticker and adhere it to the shoes, thoroughly making sure every petal edge is pressed down. Use about 12 stickers per shoe. You can place stickers over the seams of the shoes if desired—just make sure to press down as much as you can so that there's no extra space where the paint can sneak in.

4 protect the inside of the shoes. Use newspaper, an old magazine, or even paper towels to stuff the inside of the shoe so that it's protected from the paint. If desired, use painter's tape to protect other areas with more precision.

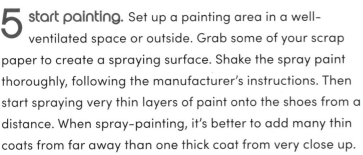

5 start painting. Set up a painting area in a well-ventilated space or outside. Grab some of your scrap paper to create a spraying surface. Shake the spray paint thoroughly, following the manufacturer's instructions. Then start spraying very thin layers of paint onto the shoes from a distance. When spray-painting, it's better to add many thin coats from far away than one thick coat from very close up.

6 finish painting. Continue until your shoes are completely and evenly covered with paint. Allow the paint to dry for several hours. When the shoes are dry to the touch, decide if they need a second coat or if you are happy with the color as is.

7

7 **remove the stickers.** Carefully remove the shoe stuffing and each sticker to reveal the pretty flowers. If you see any spots where the stencil allowed paint to sneak in where it shouldn't, touch up the spot with white fabric paint and a paintbrush.

8 **add the flower centers.** Glue a little yellow pom-pom to the center of each flower. Fabric glue works best, but you can also use regular glue or a hot glue gun. Did you know there are fabric glue sticks? How cool is that? Once the shoes themselves are done, you can add regular size pom-poms to the laces, using the same glue.

8

parrot earrings

These birds are guaranteed to bring color and good vibes wherever you go! They are the perfect handmade accessory to every outfit, adding a pop of fun. Who knew paper earrings could be so cool? Just watch out for rain— these parrots do not like water.

tip: *This is a great project for using scraps! Feel free to switch colors to make good use of any papers you already have. This project is very small, so your tiny scraps will be happy to come out and play! Remember that you will be making a pair of birds that are mirror images of each other, so complete each step once per bird using the correct template.*

tools & materials

- Template (page 181)
- Pencil
- Scissors
- Metallic cardstock in red, dark blue, and gold
- Cardstock in medium blue
- Glitter cardstock in light blue, turquoise, and black
- Glue
- Tape (optional)
- White glitter foam or glitter cardstock
- Fine-tipped black marker
- Yellow crepe paper
- Pair of stud earrings, post and back

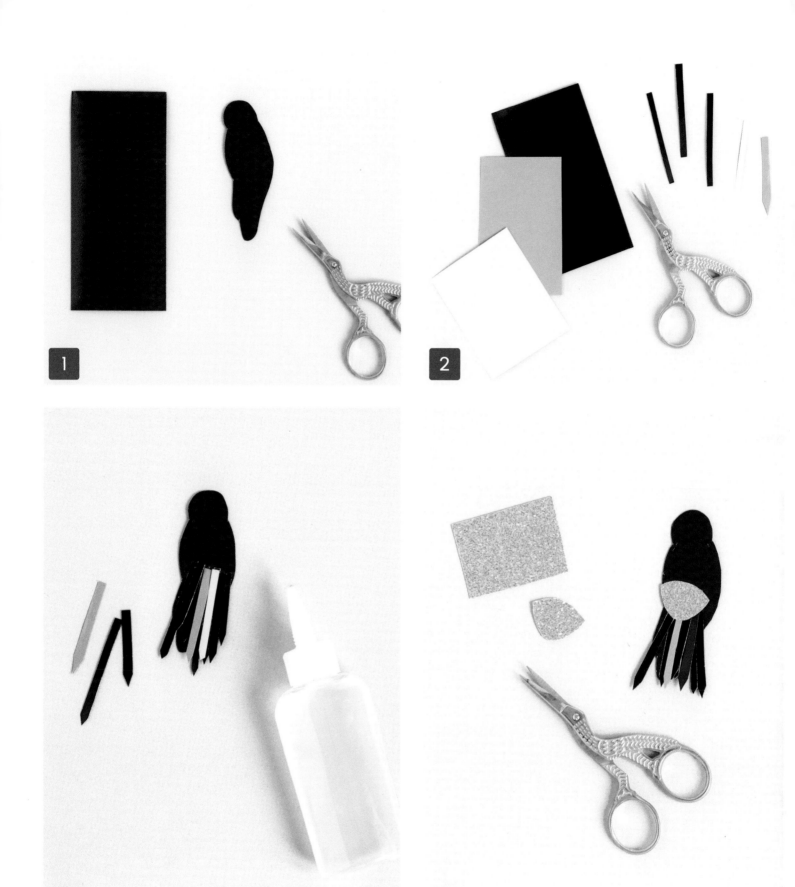

5

1 **cut the red body.** Using the template, trace and cut out the bird's body from red metallic cardstock.

2 **cut the blue tail feathers.** Using the template, trace and cut out small tail feathers from the medium blue and metallic blue cardstock. Make sure the bottoms are pointy. Cut as many pointy tail feathers as you'd like. I used between 8 and 9 per bird.

3 **attach the tail feathers.** Glue the blue tail feathers to the bird's red body.

4 **cut the belly.** Using the template, trace and cut out the belly from the light blue glitter cardstock. Glue it on top of the bird's body and tail feathers as shown.

5 **cut and attach the beak and neck.** Using the template, trace and cut out the beak and the neck. Use black glitter cardstock for the beak and gold metallic cardstock for the neck. First glue the gold neck to the red bird's head, then glue the black beak on top of the neck and the head.

6

7

6 **cut the wing feathers.** Using the template, trace and cut out small wing feathers from the light blue and turquoise glitter cardstock. Make sure the bottoms are pointy. Arrange them in a staggered manner; you can put a thin strip of tape on the back to secure the shape for later. Set these aside for now.

7 **cut the eye.** Using the template, trace and cut out a circle eye from the white glitter foam sheet. Make a little dot in the middle with a black marker to serve as a pupil. Set the eyes aside for now.

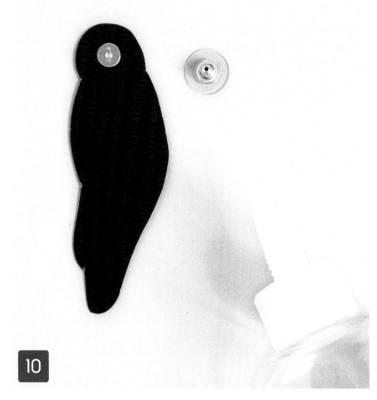

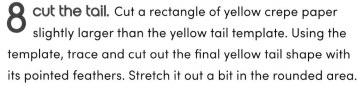

8 cut the tail. Cut a rectangle of yellow crepe paper slightly larger than the yellow tail template. Using the template, trace and cut out the final yellow tail shape with its pointed feathers. Stretch it out a bit in the rounded area.

9 attach the remaining pieces. Glue the blue wing to the side of the bird, partially overlapping the light blue belly. Glue the yellow tail on the underside of the bird. Glue the white eye on top of the beak and neck.

10 attach the earring post. Using the template, trace and cut out the bird's body from red metallic cardstock a second time. Glue the earring post to the backside, near the top. You could also poke the post through the paper and glue it; this will make it extra secure.

11 attach the backside. Glue the earring post body piece to the back of assembled earring. Get ready to wow!

banana fan

Bananas can (and should be!) everywhere—they are such a happy and tasty fruit. I still remember when I saw them for the first time on Brazilian icon Carmen Miranda's head. I mean, this *garota* knew how to have fun! We can also bring out the *tropicalísima* in us by creating this funky banana fan. If you want, play my favorite Carmen Miranda song while you're crafting: "Chica Chica Boom Chic."

tip: *Did you know there's a BANANA DAY? That's right! All banana lovers out there can celebrate their favorite fruit on the third Wednesday of April! Not that we need a day, but, you know!*

tools & materials

- Template (page 172)
- 5 sheets of 8½" x 11" (22 x 28 cm) yellow cardstock—as thick a paper weight as possible
- Scrap cardboard (such as cereal boxes, packaging, etc.)
- Pencil
- Scissors
- Pink acrylic paint
- Paintbrush
- Black marker
- Yellow or orange colored pencil
- Hole punch
- Utility knife
- Pipe cleaner
- Black thread
- Embroidery needle with a large eye
- Clear tape
- Washi tape (optional)

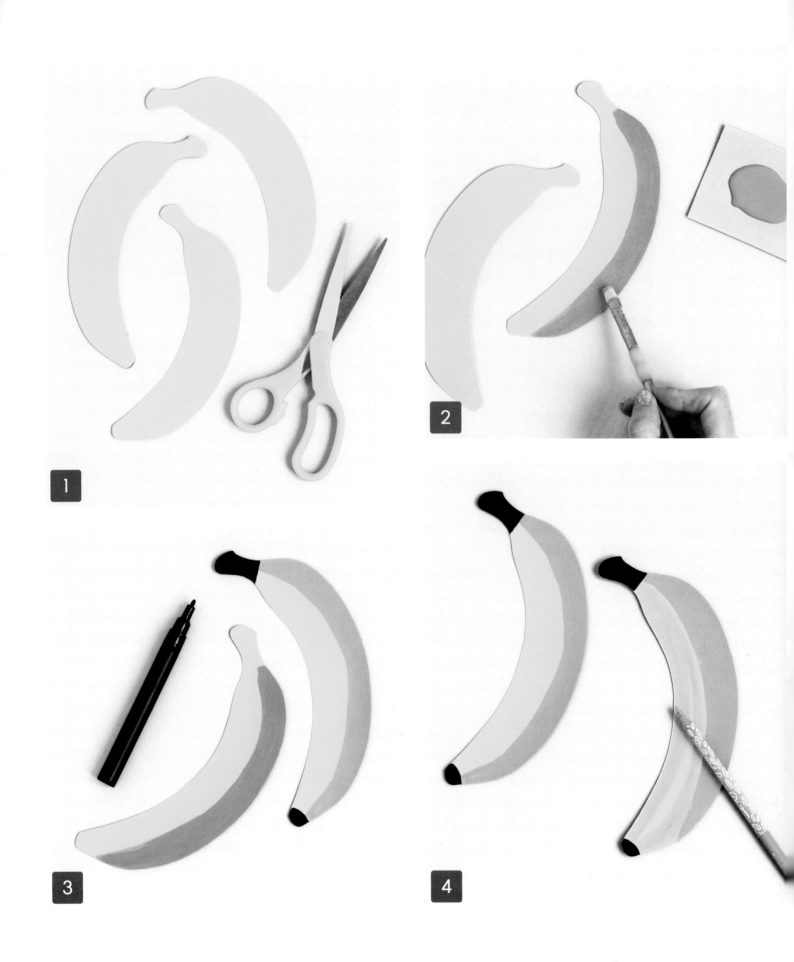

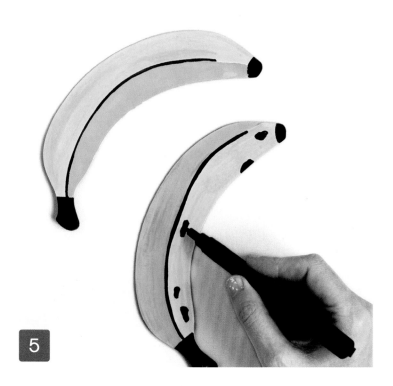

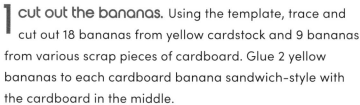

1 **cut out the bananas.** Using the template, trace and cut out 18 bananas from yellow cardstock and 9 bananas from various scrap pieces of cardboard. Glue 2 yellow bananas to each cardboard banana sandwich-style with the cardboard in the middle.

2 **paint the bananas.** Paint one side of each banana using pink acrylic paint. Mix it up—don't just paint the left sides, and don't make every pink area exactly the same shape.

3 **add black details.** Color the tip and stem of each banana using a black marker.

4 **add dimension.** Color the yellow half of each banana using a yellow or orange colored pencil (see what works best with your paper color). This adds some depth to your bananas.

5 **add more black details.** Add a centerline and some dots with black marker to incorporate some realistic detail.

6 **punch holes.** Stack all the bananas neatly on top of each other to create a single pile of bananas. Using a hole punch, make one hole where the black stem is (as shown). Your entire stack may be too thick to punch all at once, but make sure that every time you punch, all the holes are aligned.

7 **cut holes.** With a utility knife, carefully make tiny, aligned holes or cuts on the upper right section of each banana as shown. To do this, stack all the bananas again and make the first tiny hole on the first banana by pressing down and wiggling your utility knife. By doing this, you'll make a mark on the next banana in the stack. Remove the top banana, make a tiny hole using the same method in the new top banana, and continue down the stack. By keeping the bananas in a stack, your hole will always be in the same place.

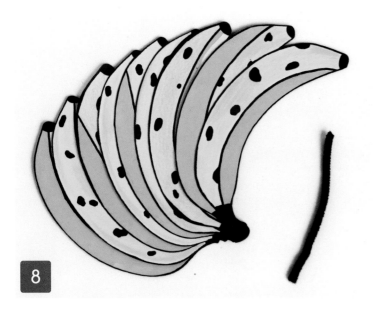

8 **tie the bananas together.** Cut a small piece of black pipe cleaner. With all the bananas stacked neatly together again, thread the pipe cleaner through the punched holes in the stems. Pinch and twist the pipe cleaner closed tight enough to be secure but loose enough for you to be able to open and close the fan.

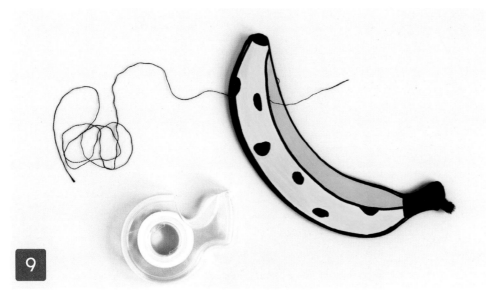

9 **thread and tape the bananas.** Cut a piece of black thread around 23" (60 cm) long. With the painted side of the banana stack facing up, start connecting all the bananas by threading through each banana hole (from front to back) until you've gone through the last one. With the bananas neatly stacked again, pull the thread almost all the way down through, leaving just a small length sticking out from the front side of the top banana. Tape this small bit of the thread down with clear tape.

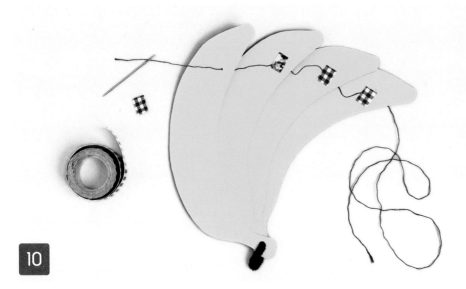

10 **tape and trim the thread.** Now turn the banana stack upside down and spread out the bananas like you would spread out a fan. Once you are happy with how your banana spread fans out, start taping the thread down on the backside of each banana so that the fan can't open up any wider than you already have it. You can do this with clear tape or washi tape like I did. Make sure the tape covers each hole.

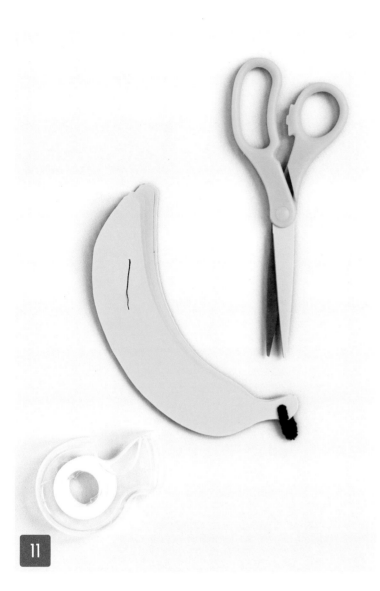

11 **finish taping.** Tape the thread down on the backside of the last banana. Cut off any excess thread. You are done! Tropicalisima for life!

confetti shoe bows

I love shoes and want them (need them?) in every color, with giant pom-poms, glitter all over, jewels on the heels—you name it! They just put a smile on my face and on my feet. If your shoes need a little extra, you'd be surprised by how easy and fun it is to accessorize them! These colorful and craftable confetti shoe bows are here to make your feet full of joy.

tip: *You can add a hair tie and transform these bows into super-cool hair accessories!*

tools & materials

- 2 quart-sized plastic freezer bags
- Rubbing alcohol
- Cotton ball
- Ruler
- Scissors
- Confetti (store-bought or custom-made)
- Small shaped hole punches (optional)
- Scrap paper (optional)
- Glitter
- Aluminum foil
- Hair straightener or clothing iron
- Gold ribbon
- Glue
- Plain metal shoe clips
- Industrial-strength adhesive (optional)

1 **de-brand the bag.** Soak a cotton ball with some rubbing alcohol and rub the brand and any other markings off the plastic bag.

2 **cut the bag.** Cut a rectangle measuring 4¾" x 3⅜" (12 x 8.5 cm) from the bottom corner of the bag, through both sides. This way, you won't have to seal more than two sides of the plastic pouch you're about to create.

3 **make and mix confetti.** Make the best confetti mixture you can think of. Use different hole punches to make circles, stars, hearts, and more from scrap paper. You can always freehand cut little pieces of paper too. Don't forget to add some glitter and gold stars. Put the confetti into the rectangle pouch.

4 **add foil to one side.** Cut a strip of aluminum foil longer than one long side of the plastic pouch. Fold the foil in half and place it over the open side, closing the edges together.

5 seal one side. Seal the edges together using a hair straightener or clothing iron on low heat. Instead of pressing with the tool, just tap down a few times for a few seconds—too much heat and pressure could melt the bag into a mess.

6 check your work. Carefully remove the foil (it may be hot) and check if the edge has sealed completely. If it hasn't, put the foil back in place and try again. Keep working with low heat and quick taps to seal the edge little by little without completely melting it. Seal the other open side as well. When it's all sealed, you can trim the sealed plastic a little bit to neaten it up.

7 tie the knot. Separate the confetti mixture inside the pouch so that there is an even amount on each side. Cut a short piece of gold ribbon, then tie a tight double knot in the middle of the rectangle.

6

7

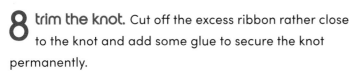

8 trim the knot. Cut off the excess ribbon rather close to the knot and add some glue to secure the knot permanently.

9 cover the knot. Use one of the trimmed pieces of excess ribbon to wrap a neat, snug circle around the knot. Glue this in place, making sure the bow isn't loose within the circle.

10 glue on the shoe clip. Place a good amount of glue all over one side of ribbon and glue the finished bow to the top side of the shoe clip. Use an extra-powerful glue for this step if possible.

upcycled wallet

This is such a cute way to carry fun around with you everywhere you go. The small project is great for stashing cash, but it would also make an adorable business card holder, don't you think? Choose a cereal box with colors and designs that you like, because they are part of the look!

tools & materials

- Cereal box
- Ruler
- Pencil
- Scissors
- Glue
- Hole punch
- Gold ribbon
- Gold swivel clasp keychain

tip: *This project is very easy to execute, but make sure you take the time to measure and fold neatly so your finished project has clean, functional lines.*

1

2

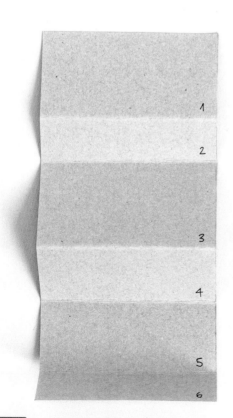

3

4

1 cut up the box. Cut apart a cereal box and trim off all the edges and flaps to get just the two big rectangles of the front and the back.

2 cut a rectangle. Choose the side of the box you like best—or make two wallets, one for a friend! Cut a rectangle measuring 4 ½" x 10" (11.5 x 25.5 cm).

3 fold the rectangle. Place the rectangle vertically on your work surface with the brown side facing up. Always starting from the top, measure and mark on both left and right sides the following measurements: 2 ⅛" (5.5 cm), 3 ½" (9 cm), 6" (15 cm), 7 ⅜" (18.8 cm), and 9" (23 cm). Draw a line between each matching set of marks as a folding guide. Label the panels 1 through 6, starting from the top panel. Then, with the brown side facing up, fold along each line: mountain fold line 1, valley fold line 2, mountain fold line 3, valley fold line 4, and valley fold line 5.

4 glue panel 2. Put glue on panel 2 and glue it down onto panel 3.

5 glue panel 4. Put glue on panel 4 and glue it down onto panel 5.

6 glue panel 6. Before gluing panel 6, fold it up onto panel 3 to check the fit. If panel 6 overlaps onto panel 1, trim off the overlap (this will remove excess bulkiness from your wallet). Then put glue on panel 6 and glue it up onto panel 3. Turn the entire thing around and you'll see that a wallet shape with two slots has formed!

7 add backing to the wallet. Cut a rectangle the same size as the rectangle you have formed by folding and gluing. Glue it onto the back of the wallet (the side with tab 1 visible).

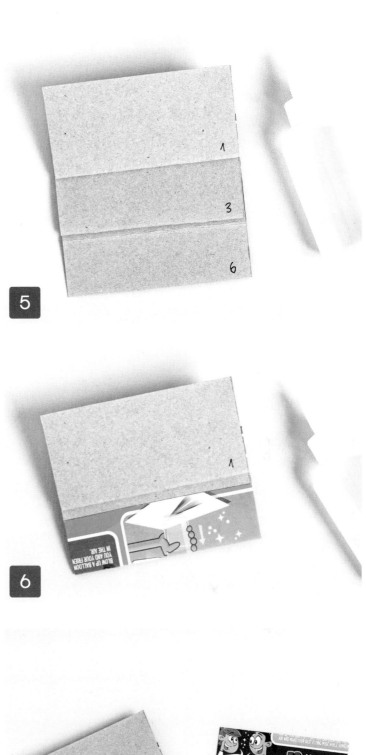

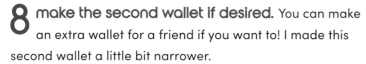

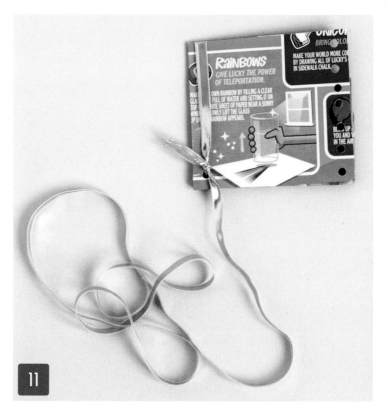

8 **make the second wallet if desired.** You can make an extra wallet for a friend if you want to! I made this second wallet a little bit narrower.

9 **punch holes.** Use a hole punch to make evenly spaced holes along both sides of the wallet. Make an uneven number of holes—I made 7: 3 on the bottom section, 2 on the middle section, and 2 on the top section.

10 **add gold ribbon.** Cut a piece of ribbon about 24 ½" (62 cm) long. Starting from the backside of the bottom hole, thread gold ribbon up through the hole and back down through the next hole in the column. Continue weaving up the entire side of the wallet until the ribbon is coming out of the top hole.

11 **tie one side.** Flip the wallet around to the backside, fold the ribbon neatly down over the top of the wallet, and tie the end securely to the ribbon at the bottom hole, right where it comes out from the hole.

12 **weave the other side.** Bring the loose end of the ribbon across the back of the wallet to thread it through the other side's bottom hole to the front. Weave the ribbon up this side of the wallet just like you did the first side.

13 **finish the wallet.** Once you've reached the top, bring the ribbon back down over the top edge and tie it the bottom the same way you did the first side. Trim any excess ribbon. Add the keychain to the hole in one top corner, and you're ready to roll!

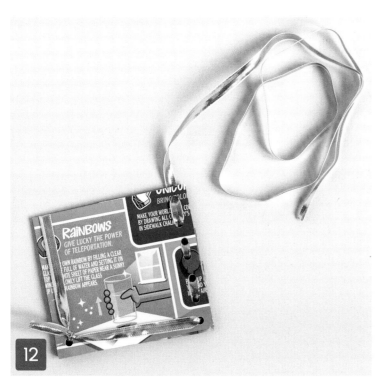

heart scrunchies

Accessories are the most fun way to add pizzazz to any outfit, and these little ponytail holders are no exception. Just grab your favorite silicone mold (I'm thinking cats for Halloween, little trees for the winter holidays, and hearts all year round) and glue away! You can go as wild as you want with the add-ons. Have you seen how the always-fun Iris Apfel rocks her accessories? Never too much, never too many!

tip: *This is a great project for using up larger charms that you just love but haven't been able to figure out a use for.*

tools & materials

- Silicone mold (I used a heart-shaped mold)
- Hot glue gun
- Confetti
- Glitter
- Small gems, buttons, beads, and charms
- Hair elastics

1 **prep for the project.** Choose your favorite silicone mold. Put all the add-ins you want to include in this scrunchie within arm's reach, and think about how you want to arrange the items. Once you start dispensing the glue, you'll want to work relatively quickly.

2 **add glue to the mold.** Heat up a glue gun with a glue stick in place. Once the glue is very hot, fill up the mold with glue to your desired thickness. It doesn't necessarily have to be the entire depth of the mold.

3 **add confetti.** Sprinkle confetti into the mold.

4 **add glitter.** Add glitter into the mold.

5 **add gems and other items.** Add any magical add-ins you have into the mold. I like to include cute buttons, miniatures, small charms, beads, and more. If you want to be extra careful, use a small, pointed utensil to gently press the item into the glue while keeping your fingers clear of it.

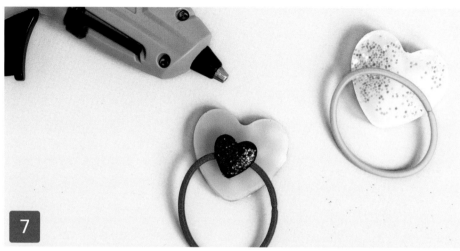

6 add the hair elastic. Once the glue has fully dried and cooled enough to touch, remove the shape from the mold. Turn the shape around to the backside and glue a section of a hair elastic to the center of the shape.

7 add the finishing touch. Use more hot glue to attach a button, a three-dimensional sticker, or even a piece of thick scrap paper on top of the hair elastic where it meets the molded shape. Be careful not to burn yourself—use your pressing utensil again if needed.

8 make more scrunchies. Make a thematic set of scrunchies one at a time until you have enough for any hairdo!

muchas gracias!

WOW! SO many people have made this book possible that I don't even know where to start!

To my childhood friend and partner in craft, Delfi, who came all the way from Argentina to help me plan and create all the projects in this book! Not only was she so much fun to craft with, but her right-to-the-point personality was just what I needed to get started when this book was a big, blank, scary page! Thank you, Delfi, for joining me in this wild once-in-a-lifetime adventure! Or, wait . . . should we make Part 2? Vamaaasss! A craftearla en Miami! Esta vez con gin et tonics!

To my sidekick, yes girl, and photographer, Gaby, thank you! You are always lifting me up and reminding me that we can do a-ny-thing! Working together on this book has been a dream come true. The amount of love and dedication you've put into this is shown in every photo you've taken. This wouldn't have happened without you! Que decirte Grace, tu empuje es TODO. Gracias por subirte a este proyecto y hacerlo tan tuyo!

To Pato, the amazing art stylist of this book, thank you for creating the most magical scenes for my craft projects. Thank you for your commitment and for making me feel like this was the most important book you ever worked for. You went above and beyond to make everything so special—and you nailed it! I could not be happier with the final result. Gracias por la magia, Pato, y por dejarme tirar estrellitas por todos lados!

LAS QUIERO!

A very special thank you to:

Delfi del Carril, Nele de Selva de Papel, Mili Pini, Sofi Tagle, Loli Mallea, Romi Connell de Rainbow Factory, Sofi de Letiti Tortas, Car Pintos, Luis de Floreria Regia Casa, Pani es Delicioso de Martinez, Sebastián Atienza de Cacho Rotiseria, El bus de Otto, Labán Pâtisserie, Calesita de Ecoparque, Laura Martín.

Thank you to my friends, my family, and all of those who support my work every day on social media. I may not know all of you in person, but believe me, your support and buenas ondas have made this book possible too!

Thank you to my amazing publisher, Peg, her incredible editor, Colleen, and everyone who has worked so hard on this book!

templates

Every template in this section is meant to be traced one or more times on your chosen type of paper (cardstock, glitter paper, crepe paper, tissue paper, etc.).

The template pages are perforated to make it easy for you to remove a sheet and neatly photocopy it. Then, cut out the template shape from the photocopy. (The template pages are printed on both sides, so you don't want to cut up the original page.) If desired, you can trace the shape onto something thicker than printer paper, like a thin piece of cardboard, to make it easier to trace many times.

If you need extras or simply don't want to remove pages, you can print the templates at home at the following link: www.betterdaybooks.com/big-book-of-happy-crafts-templates-download

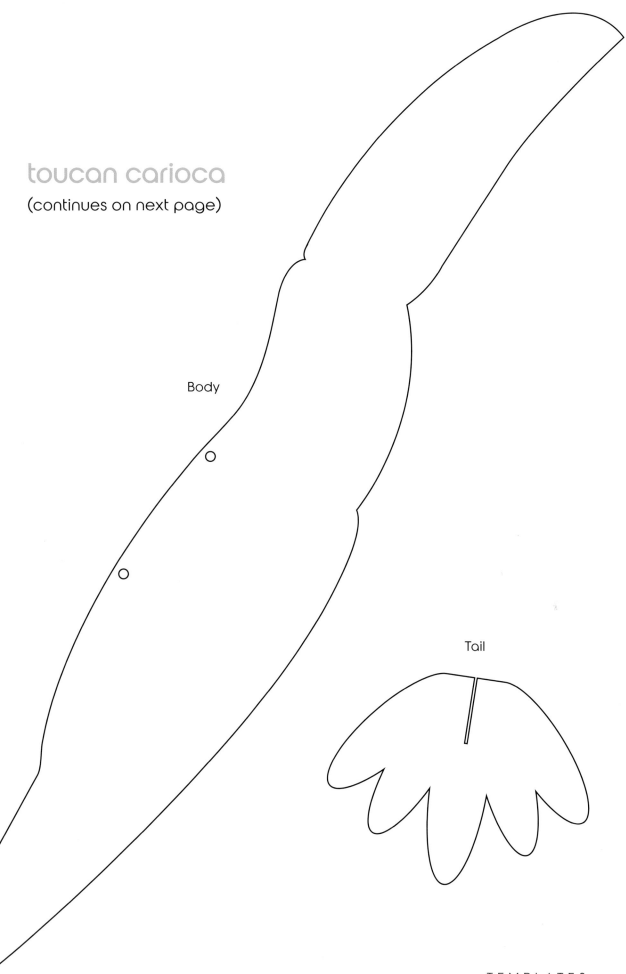

toucan carioca
(continues on next page)

Body

Tail

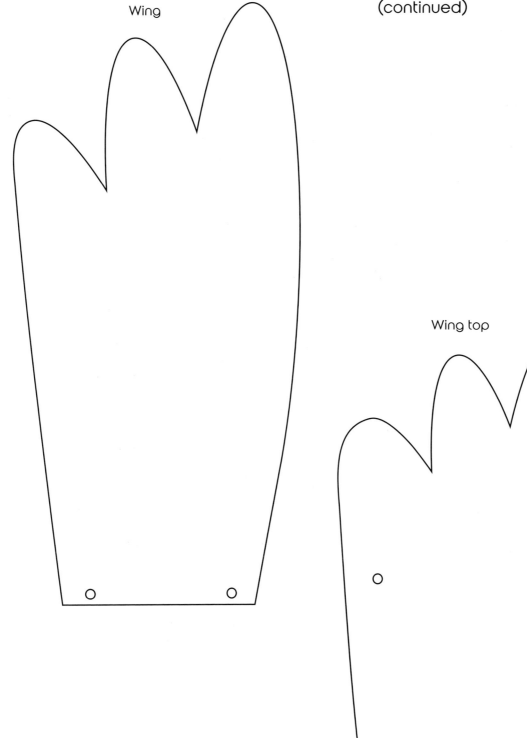

Wing

Wing top

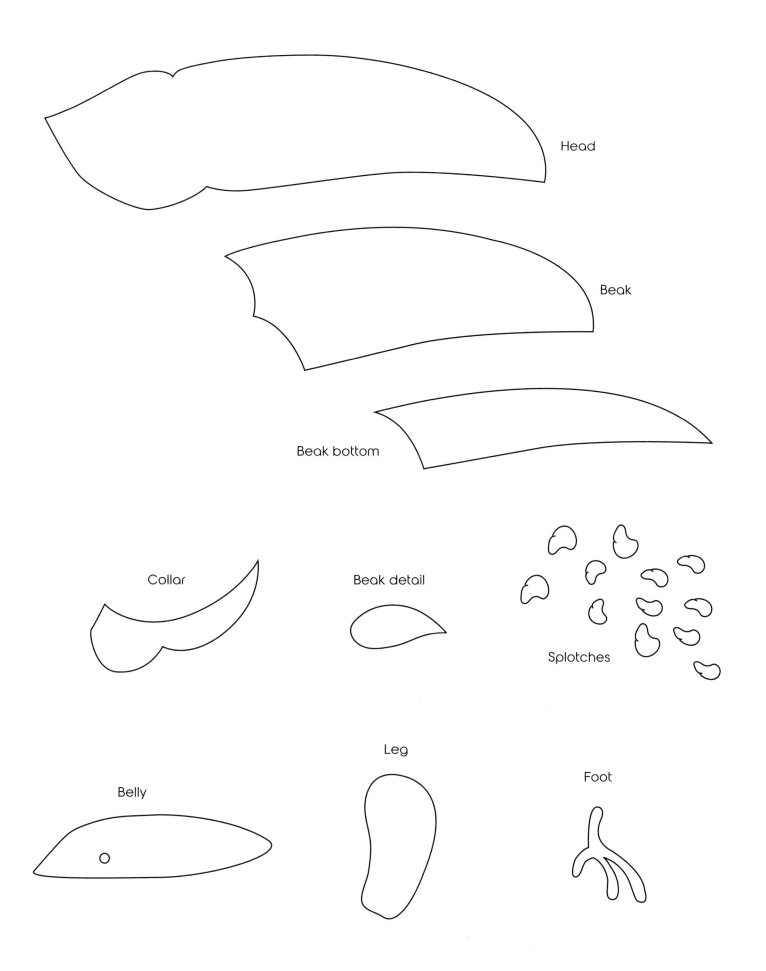

Head

Beak

Beak bottom

Collar

Beak detail

Splotches

Belly

Leg

Foot

banana fan

cake stand

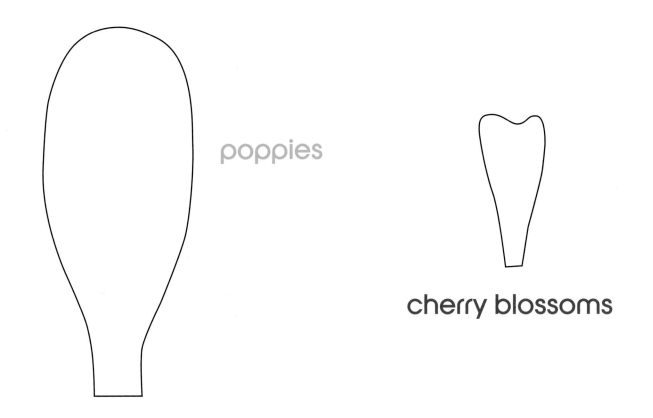

poppies

cherry blossoms

flower
curtain

paper chandelier **& butterfly crown** (butterfly only)

tropical chandelier

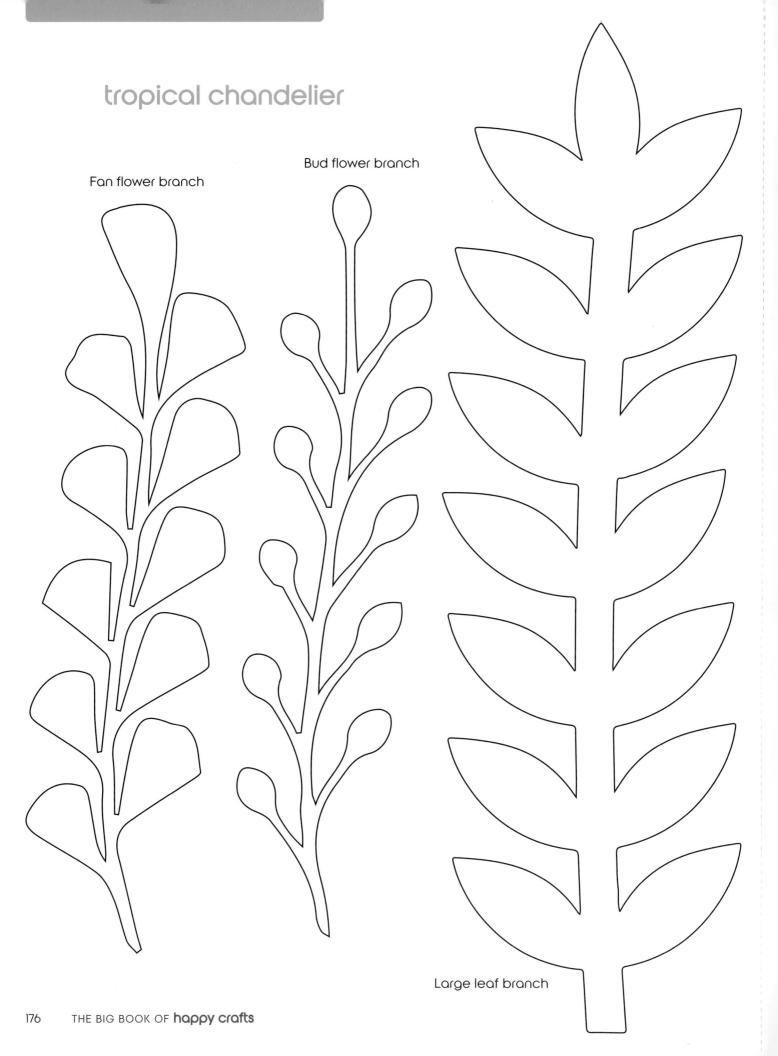

Fan flower branch

Bud flower branch

Large leaf branch

Medium leaf branch

9-petal flower

4-petal flower

leaf wreath

THE BIG BOOK OF **happy crafts**

sunflowers

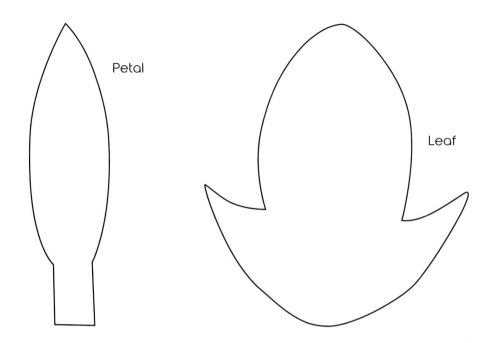

Petal

Leaf

forever plant (continues on next page)

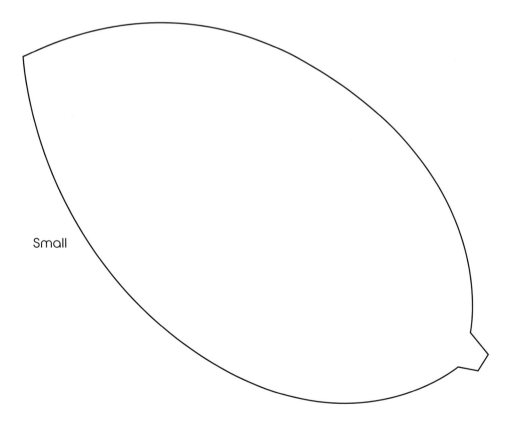

Small

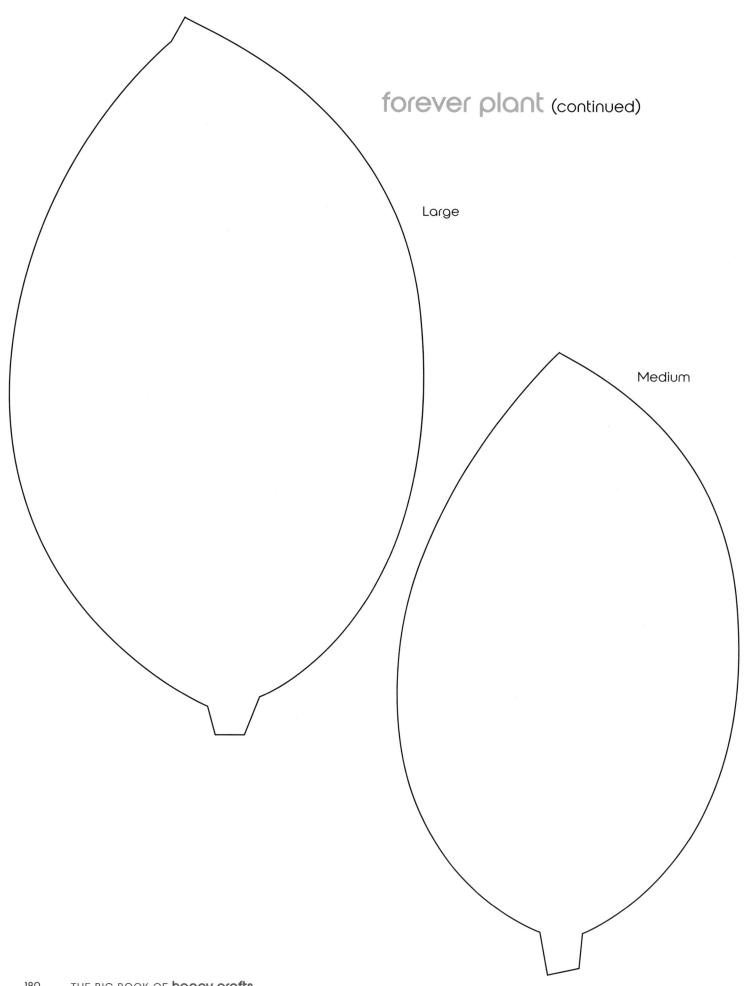

forever plant (continued)

Large

Medium

parrot earrings

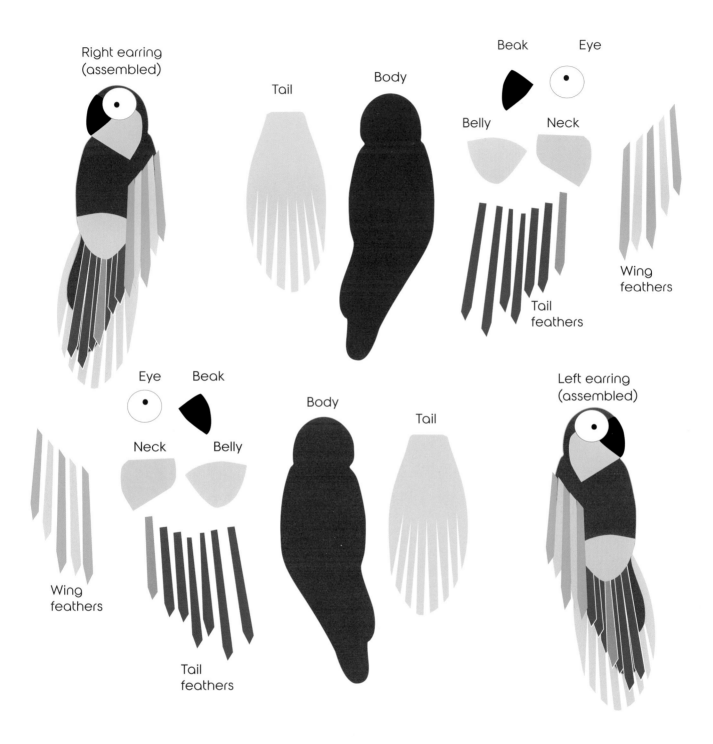

Right earring
(assembled)

Tail

Body

Beak

Eye

Belly

Neck

Wing
feathers

Tail
feathers

Eye

Beak

Neck

Belly

Body

Tail

Left earring
(assembled)

Wing
feathers

Tail
feathers

Index

Note: Page numbers in *italics* indicate projects and templates. Page range with an asterisk (*) indicates ready-to-use Pullout Goodies

A
acrylic paint, 17

B
Banana Fan, *145–49 (172)*
bows, confetti shoe, *151–55*
Butterfly Crown, *89–91 (175)*

C
Cake Stand, *67–71 (172)*
candles, confetti, *73–75*
chandeliers
  Paper Chandelier, *55–59 (175)*
  Tropical Chandelier, *45–49
    (176–77)*
Cherry Blossoms, *95–99 (174)*
colors
  samples (Pantone numbers),
    18–19
  using, 18
confetti
  Confetti Candles, *73–75*
  Confetti Purse, *127–31*
  Confetti Shoe Bows, *151–55*
  Party Poppers, *83–87*
crafts and crafting. *See
    also* décor projects; flower
    projects; party projects;
    projects
  about: author's background
    and studio overview, 10–13
  color samples (Pantone
    numbers), 18–19
  color use, 18
  creativity and self-expression,
    20–21
  maker's mantra, 20
  reusing and upcycling
    materials, 22
  supplies for (*See* tools and
    materials)
  templates for, 22–23
  tips/recommendations for,
    22–23
creativity and self-expression,
    20–21
crowns
  Butterfly Crown, *89–91 (175)*
  Party Crown, *77–81*
curtain, flower, *61–63 (174)*
customizing projects, 21

D
décor projects, 25–63
  Flower Curtain, *61–63 (174)*
  Leaf Wreath, *33–37 (178)*
  Palm Leaves, *39–43*
  Paper Chandelier, *55–59 (175)*
  Statement Stars, *51–53*
  Toucan Carioca, *27–31
    (169–71)*, 185–91*
  Tropical Chandelier, *45–49
    (176–77)*

E
earrings, parrot, *139–43 (181)*

F
fan, banana, *145–49 (172)*
flower projects, 93–123
  Cherry Blossoms, *95–99 (174)*
  Flower Curtain, *61–63 (174)*
  Flower Shoes, *133–37 (173)*
  Forever Plant, *107–11 (179–80)*
  Giant Flower, *101–5*
  Poppies, *113–17 (174)*
  Sunflowers, *119–23 (179)*
  Forever Plant, *107–11 (179–80)*

G
Giant Flower, *101–5*
glitter, 17
glue, 16

H
Heart Scrunchies, *163–67*

hole punch, 17

L
Leaf Wreath, *33–37 (178)*

P
paints, 17
paper, 16
Paper Chandelier, *55–59 (175)*
paper trimmer, 17
Parrot Earrings, *139–43 (181)*
party projects, 65–91
  Butterfly Crown, *89–91 (175)*
  Cake Stand, *67–71 (172)*
  Confetti Candles, *73–75*
  Party Crown, *77–81*
  Party Poppers, *83–87*
plants. *See* flower projects
Poppies, *113–17 (174)*
projects. *See also* décor
  projects; party projects; style
  projects
  author's background and,
    10–11
  customizing, 21
  getting ready for, 22
  getting started, 15
  recommendations for, 22
  supplies for (*See* tools and
    materials)
  templates for, 22–23
pullout goodies, Toucan
  Carioca, 185–91*
purse, confetti, *127–31*

R
reusing and upcycling
  materials, 22
ribbon, 17

S
scissors, 16
scrunchies, heart, *163–67*

self-expression, creativity and,
    20–21
shoes, flower, *133–37 (173)*
Statement Stars, *51–53*
style projects, 125–67
  Banana Fan, *145–49 (172)*
  Confetti Purse, *127–31*
  Confetti Shoe Bows, *151–55*
  Flower Shoes, *133–37 (173)*
  Heart Scrunchies, *163–67*
  Parrot Earrings, *139–43 (181)*
  Upcycled Wallet, *157–61*
Sunflowers, *119–23 (179)*

T
tape, types to stock, 17
templates, using, 22–23, 168.
  See also specific projects
  (references in parentheses)
tools and materials, 16–17
  acrylic paint, 17
  glitter, 17
  glue, 16
  hole punch, 17
  keeping them tidy, 22
  paper, 16
  paper trimmer, 17
  ribbon and twine, 17
  scissors, 16
  tape (types to stock), 17
  Toucan Carioca, 169–71,
    185–91*
  Tropical Chandelier, *45–49
    (176–77)*
  twine, 17

U
Upcycled Wallet, *157–61*
upcycling materials, 21

W
wallet, upcycled, *157–61*
wreath, leaf, *33–37 (178)*

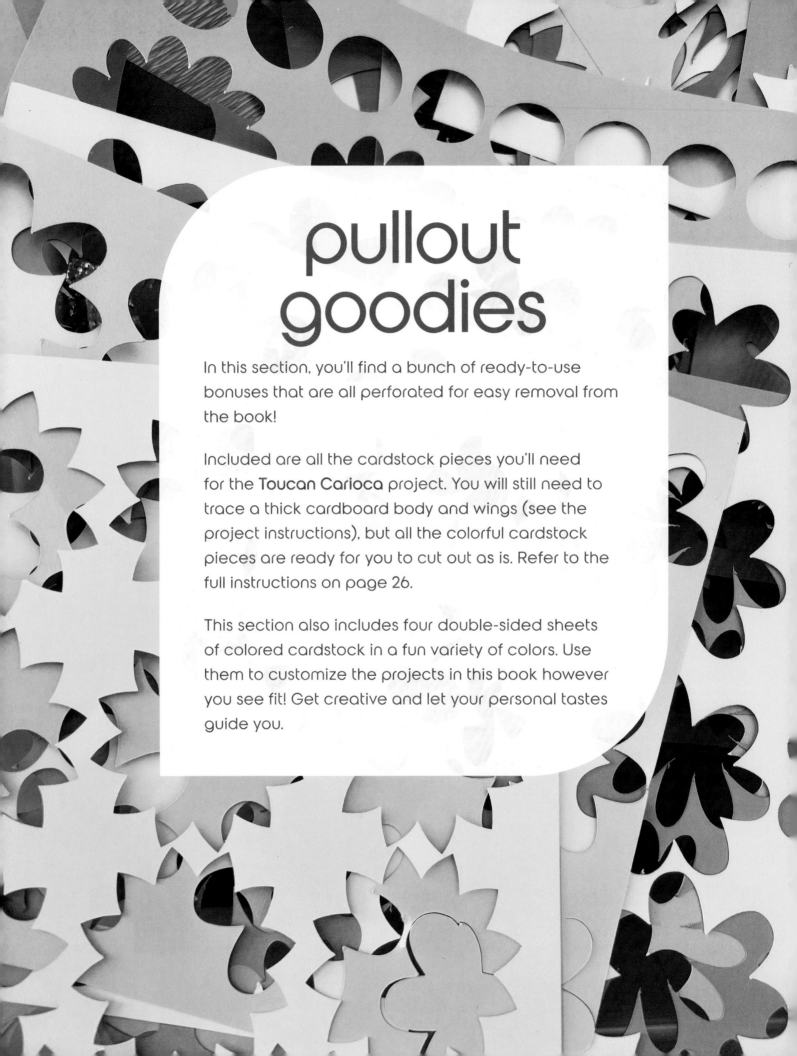

pullout goodies

In this section, you'll find a bunch of ready-to-use bonuses that are all perforated for easy removal from the book!

Included are all the cardstock pieces you'll need for the **Toucan Carioca** project. You will still need to trace a thick cardboard body and wings (see the project instructions), but all the colorful cardstock pieces are ready for you to cut out as is. Refer to the full instructions on page 26.

This section also includes four double-sided sheets of colored cardstock in a fun variety of colors. Use them to customize the projects in this book however you see fit! Get creative and let your personal tastes guide you.

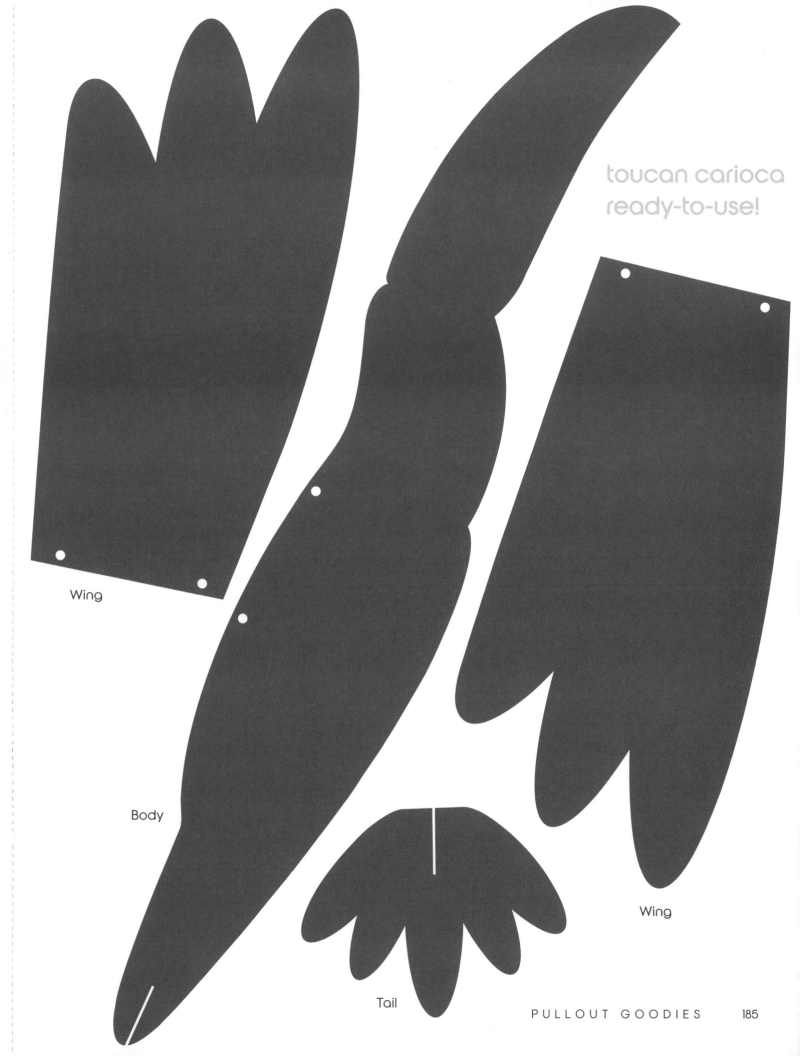

toucan carioca
ready-to-use!

Wing

Body

Tail

Wing

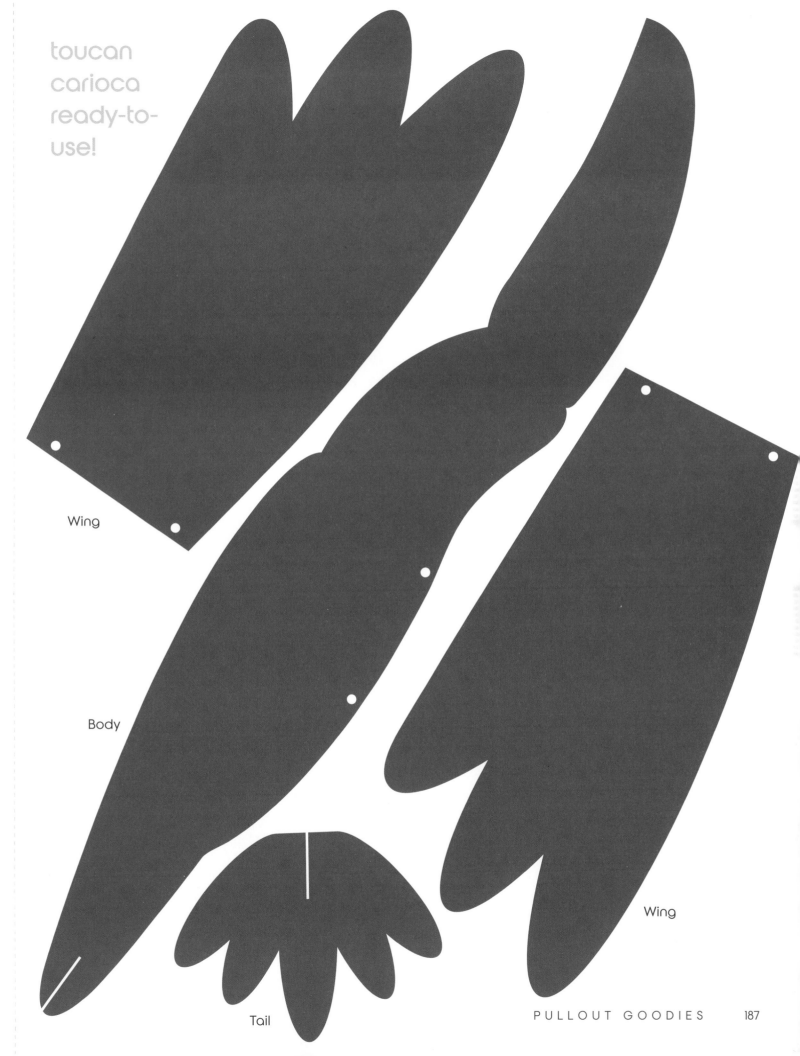

toucan
carioca
ready-to-
use!

Wing

Body

Tail

Wing

toucan carioca ready-to-use!

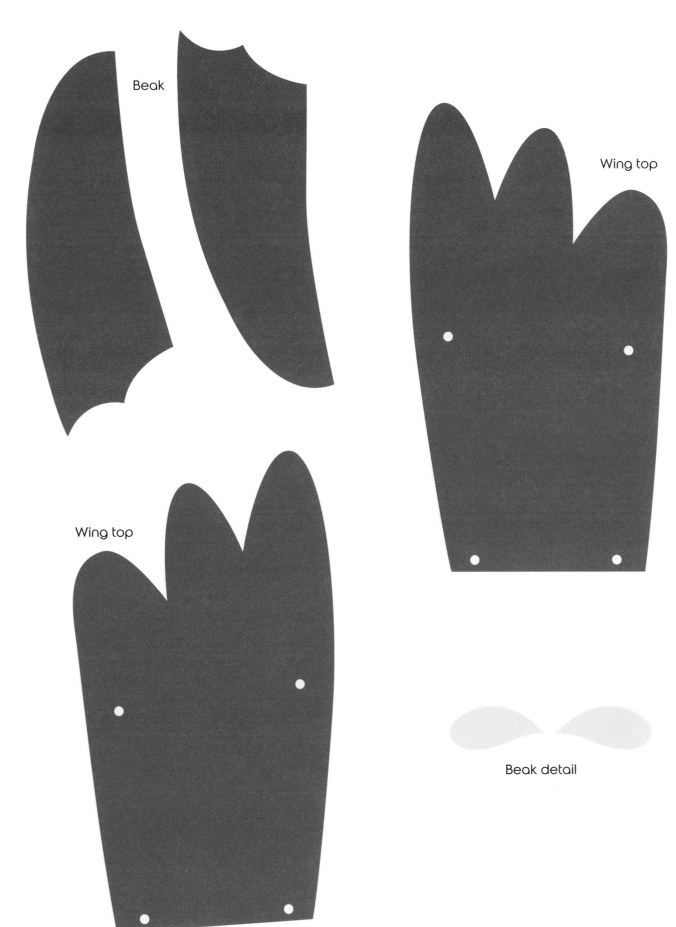

Beak

Wing top

Wing top

Beak detail

toucan carioca ready-to-use!

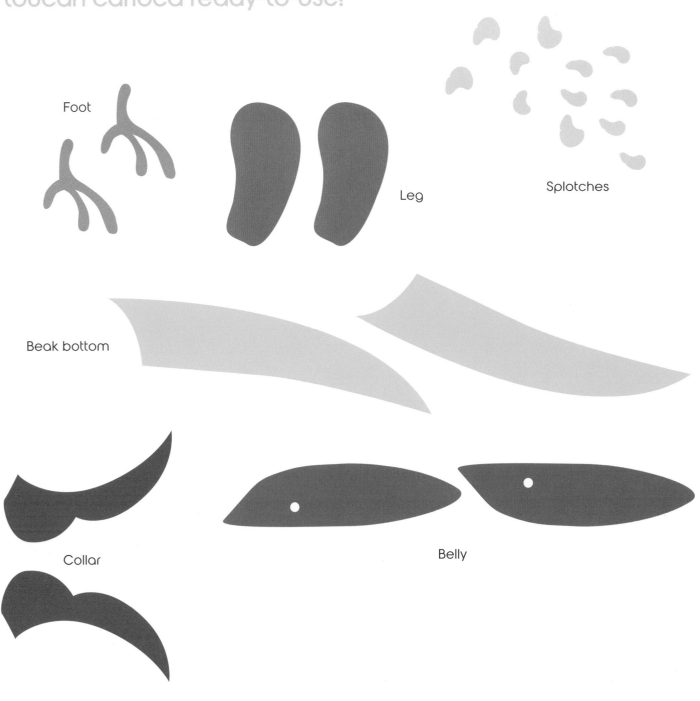

Foot

Leg

Splotches

Beak bottom

Collar

Belly

Head

This is the backside of the Leg and Foot pieces! Cut out the shapes from the other side of this sheet like normal. ▶

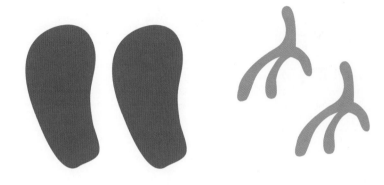